SECRETS FROM
THE LITTLE RED BOX

JAE CARVEL

Cover Design by Gwen Gades
Edited by Mary Ward Menke

This is a work of fi ction. Names, characters, places, brands, media, and incidents are either the product of the author's i magination or are used fi ctitiously. Any resemblance to similarly named places or to persons living or deceased is unintentional.

Library of Congress Control Number: 2016904890

DEDICATION

To Jean

The Strawberry Mountain Series
By the River
Secrets from the Little Red Box

FOREWORD

Mountains, mines, and Model Ts create a backdrop for Evelyn's and Harry's correspondence. The letters that inspired this novel are authentic to the time period and to the people who wrote them.

The characters are descended from the stalwart pioneers who left their homes and settled in Oregon. Their children are venturing into the 20th century as independent forward thinkers, restrained by their 19th century upbringing, but determined to push ahead.

The little red box that contained Harry's letters was tucked away in the attic of the ranch house before 1920 and was recovered seventy-five years later.

With the letters, a primary source of historical information, and my own imagination I have attempted to show the reader a true picture of the early 20th century.

JC

Prologue

INTERRUPTION

Evelyn called up her best friend, Daisy Brown. "Daisy, get your gear together. We are going to Portland!" said Evelyn. "I'm going to look into finishing my schooling. My ma and I spent a lot of time discussing what life would be like for an educated woman. That was what she had expected of me, and I plan to fill the role. She believed women should not have to depend on men, that they should be self-sufficient. I plan to meet the goals we had set for me. Ma's spirit is still pretty strong around this place."

"Well, sure, let's go! I am tired of seeing you lump around. Twenty-year-olds need to be on the go. This is the 20th century. Time to read the papers, shed the corsets, get fancy hats, kid gloves just for dressing up, and get ourselves noticed." One could always count on Daisy to stir up a good time.

"I'll check with my brother George to be sure he can look in on Pa every day in case he needs something."

Fortunately, Pa's and George's ranches stood side by side. Evelyn had helped George and Alice when their son was born. Now she figured they could help her out as she finished her dream of an advanced education. Right now, a trip to the city out of this valley was what Evelyn needed!

Two years had passed since Evelyn's mother died. Evelyn was 19 at the time, the youngest child in the family. She came home from school in Portland to attend the funeral. It seemed that she cried more than anyone else in the family. The Martins were ones to keep their emotions in check. Evelyn could hardly imagine where all the tears came from. After a while she just felt sad and cheated. She and Ma had made plans for her future. Her brothers and sisters had wives, husbands, and homes of their own. Ma had devoted herself to Evelyn's rearing and education. She believed women of the 20th century should be independent, able to care for themselves. That is why the Martins sent Evelyn to business school in Portland. Ma's sudden death interrupted the plans. Evelyn harbored feelings of guilt because she resented the death as well as feeling sad about missing her mother. Then one day, her grief vanished. She could not explain it, but she knew it was time to move ahead—time to call Daisy.

Conveniently, Pa and brother George had taken on a new project, a small herd of purebred shorthorns. Caring for the 20 head of cows required complete recordkeeping for each one. To Evelyn's surprise the two men had named each cow: Bessie, Flossie, Blanche, Rose, Paleface, etc. She knew when calves came in the spring, a numbering system would go into effect, but George's wife Alice could help with the records required for the purebreds.

Pa owned a small percentage of the Imperial Hotel in Portland. He was losing his passion for this investment, and Evelyn imagined she could take over some of the responsibilities for him since she would be in Portland as she finished school. It seems sometimes an interruption in plans opens doors for new beginnings.

Evelyn and Daisy enjoyed a week of fun in the city, shopping, having lunch with old classmates, seeing the current musical show. Arrangements were made for Evelyn to finish her school courses. She slipped back into the social swing of her classmates. Daisy felt inspired to go into business and took the train back to Prairie City with plans to open a hat and notions shop. Evelyn's studies went very well as she had a propensity for numbers and her experience with recordkeeping held her in good stead.

Spending time in the city exposed Evelyn to the culture of the times. Her friend Rich Shearer and his sister Letty included her in their social affairs. She met adventurers and businessmen, college graduates and landowners. She began her business school career wearing white Gibson Girl blouses, starched and pressed and tucked into the waistband of her long black skirt. By the time she finished her courses, she owned a fashionable tailored suit. Skirts were less full and a bit shorter. Hats of smaller proportion suited Evelyn, dainty and small as she was.

Taking classes and internships had kept her in Portland for three years, but now it was time to go home to the ranch.

HARRY

Harry Smithworth felt smothered in England at the end of the century. His home, a perfectly acceptable place to live, lacked the excitement he looked for. The girl he thought he loved chose his brother Stewart as her future husband. His touch of shyness kept him from speaking up for himself. After the wedding, Harry pooled his resources and investigated a voyage to America. His good-bye to his family was replaced with the excitement of the ship's sailing. He knew his education would hold him in good stead in the new world. A mining engineer in the British Isles found himself dealing with coal and all the troubles of the miners. Harry believed his skills were destined to be used in the western United States, where miners searched for gold to fulfill their dreams.

Harry made his way across the continent, finally arriving in California. The stories of gold were just that, unsubstantiated stories, and he soon found himself on his way to Oregon. Portland was the largest city and offered some entertainment. It was, however, Harry's jumping off place for more mining adventures. He spent time acquainting himself with other men whose interests were the same as his. As his finances dwindled, he found it important to make connections in the mining industry as well as with a good banker, namely his acquaintance, Richard Shearer.

Harry slipped the crook of his umbrella over the back of the extra chair as he entered the dining room of the Imperial Hotel on the corner of 4th and Broadway in downtown Portland, Oregon. Horse-drawn vehicles jockeyed with the newer motor cars taking street space. He was glad to be inside out of the pelting rain. He rarely thought of England anymore, but an Oregon rain provided a trigger point for his memories.

"Damn, it's pouring, and I left my umbrella at the bank!" Richard complained as he adjusted himself into the vacant seat at Harry's table.

Harry responded in his pleasant British accent, which intrigued Richard as he listened. "This is Oregon rain, different from the drizzle I left in England so many years ago."

"Are you making plans for the future? I checked your account at the bank. Your funds are diminishing," Richard shared his thoughts.

"You are telling me what I already know. I can't say that I want to face up to it, but gold mining claws at me and I still hope to strike it rich. My current fund would not buy property, my other desire. It looks like mining is the way to go in hopes of earning enough to purchase land in the future," Harry explained.

"Will you be spending time here in Portland while you get your affairs in order?"

"Absolutely! I have been on the road too long. It's time for some culture and meeting people, especially a lady or two. You know I left a lovely young woman in England who married my brother. I have finally come to terms with it; water over the dam as they say." As Harry spoke, the waiter came to take their order.

As the gentlemen finished their meal, Harry nudged Richard. "Say, Rich, there is a lovely little lady at the table

across the room She has been there some time. Do you suppose her escort is just late, or decided not to come?"

Richard's gaze fell on Evelyn. "That is Evelyn Martin.
She is an acquaintance of my sister Letty. They were in business school together. I think she handles her father's interest
in this hotel. Now that the rain has let up, I must head home,
but we could sidle across the room on our way out and I
could give you an introduction."

EVELYN

Evelyn had popped inside the dining room to avoid the Western Oregon rain and wind that blew in her face. The streetcar ride from her school apartment on the hill began on a clear afternoon. She disembarked on 6th Avenue, where she planned to stroll to Broadway for some window shopping. The sudden downpour overwhelmed her umbrella, so she stepped into the Imperial dining room, even though she was early for her appointment with Mr. Payne, the hotel manager.

Pa's interest in the Imperial Hotel had been purchased in the 1880s when he had taken a trip to Portland to enroll his twin boys in school. When her mother died, his interest in the hotel waned and he considered selling. That was when Evelyn said, "Pa, I can check on the affairs of the hotel for you while I attend school. It will keep you informed and I will gain practical business experience as well."

"Well, Evie, I suppose it would work. My interest has drooped since Ma passed, but I know she wanted you to get a fine education and put it to good use; she was determined you would not have to depend on marriage to be cared for."

Today was the time for the regular meeting with the manager. A dinner meeting had been planned for 6:00 p.m. as she would be leaving Portland in a few months to return home to the ranch.

Evelyn ordered hot tea to stave off the results of the cold wind and rain and removed her precious kid gloves and put them in her handbag, which was large enough to hold a few legal papers.

The set time for dinner was an hour away, so she looked over the familiar contracts. Her mind strayed as she glanced about the room. White tablecloths were set with napkins and heavy flatware. What could have been an intimate room appeared spacious because of the large mirrors mounted on the west wall above the wainscoting.

Evelyn noticed a gentleman seated alone across the room. He ordered something to drink from the waiter and appeared to be waiting for a companion. She occupied herself noting the various parties coming in to dine, but realized she must be staring when the waiter asked if she would like to order from the menu.

"Please just refill my tea. I have a dinner appointment with Mr. Payne at 6:00. The rain drove me inside early," explained Evelyn. The waiter nodded as he went to retrieve hot tea. *If I were home on the ranch,* she thought, *it would be time for supper. Our midday meal is dinner, a sturdy meal designed to let the men get back to productive afternoon work. I wouldn't be wearing my new dove gray suit either.*

The suit was the latest good style, with the skirt shorter and partially hidden under the fashionable longer-than-hip-length jacket. She knew the women in Prairie City would be wearing skirts above the ankles because they were easier for working and getting about, not because of fashion. Evelyn could feel a bit of nostalgia for the ranch in the John Day Valley. *Yes, it will be time to go home in the spring,* she told herself.

"Evelyn, how are you?" asked Richard Shearer, who had walked up behind her table.

"I am just fine; avoiding the rain, as you can see," she answered.

"My friend and I have just finished a fine meal," he explained. "May I introduce Harry Smithworth . . . Miss Evelyn Martin," said Richard.

Harry explained what a pleasure it was to meet Evelyn and after a bit of idle conversation, he and Richard expressed their interest in having a dinner together one day soon. Richard promised to check on a date that would be good for Letty. Evelyn nodded in agreement.

After the men left, Evelyn thought about the plans. She was hoping they would choose Jake's Crawfish for dinner. It was one of her favorite eateries. Its specialty was seafood, something no restaurant in the John Day Valley would serve. To catch one's own trout in the river was the best fish to be had at home.

*   *   *

The dinner at Jake's was delicious and successful. Harry and Evelyn "hit it off," as they say. Evelyn found the company of the refined Englishman most pleasant. Harry found the savvy young ranch woman who knew something about the mining possibilities in the John Day Valley in Eastern Oregon exactly to his liking. Both of them felt there might be a future between them. Of course, neither one said so aloud.

Harry did contact her a few days later. He suggested a buggy ride up the canyon and into the rose gardens on the west hills of Portland. They reminded him of the English gardens of his home and inspired him to tell Evelyn about himself, his family, his childhood. It seemed since leaving England, he had not shared his past life with anyone.

Evelyn listened intently, enjoying his gentle accent when he spoke. She wondered how he would be received in Eastern Oregon should he come to visit her. Timing seemed right for a lasting friendship to develop.

When the time came for Evelyn to go home to the ranch for the summer, Harry tried to find a good reason to go to the same area for mining. Near Baker City he heard about the Greenhorn area and the Sumpter Valley strike. Then there was the Dixie Mine near Prairie City. Harry figured he could knock around Oregon for a couple of years looking for gold. He also figured spending time with Evelyn would make his gold hunting more fun. She took the train home the end of June. Richard and Letty usually saw Evelyn to the train, but this year Harry escorted her to the depot and planted a firm kiss as he saw her off, with promises to call on her when he came east of the mountains. The train ride to Baker City gave her plenty of time to think about her Englishman friend. She wondered if Pa would like him if he did come to call. Her mother's family had all come to the United States from England in an earlier generation. Maybe that led her to be so comfortable around Harry. She rode the stage to Austin Junction where George and Pa picked her up in the hack. Evelyn wondered if it wasn't time to add a Model T to the ranch's equipment.

SECRETS FROM
THE LITTLE RED BOX

This old box is worn on the edges and popping loose on three corners. I mend it immediately with crinkly masking tape, ruining any antique value it may have. Now I take a sip of my coffee and my first serious peek inside. Neatly stacked and folded, in chronological order, are letters to Evelyn from Harry.

Secrets from the Little Red Box

CHAPTER ONE

Evelyn pulled her buggy to a dusty stop in front of the house after driving home from town where she had gone to pick up the mail in the afternoon. The mail was delivered to Prairie City residents by the Sumpter Valley Railroad, which traversed on the newly finished track from Baker City, Oregon. Across the driveway, Pa was stooped over in the garden, hoeing the lettuce rows and the peas to encourage a good crop. She unharnessed Benson, her favorite horse for buggy rides, and turned him into the corral.

In the kitchen, Evelyn stacked bills and other mail on the corner of the oversized table that Pa had built forty years ago for his family. Ma and Evelyn's eight brothers and sisters had dined in the big square kitchen at the hand-hewn table throughout the late 1800s. Now Pa and Evelyn had their meals at the east end of the table, just the two of them, except during haying or other times when hired help was needed.

Evelyn managed the bookkeeping and check writing for the running of the ranch using the west end of the table as her desk, clearing the papers away when extra space was needed. The file box on the counter held the land deeds and homestead papers of all the pieces of land Pa had purchased to add to his ranch. Today, a personal letter drew her attention. The return address of Galice, Oregon told her it was a letter from Harry. She stretched for the well-worn letter opener stowed in a green pot on the kitchen counter and sliced it open.

> *Galice, Oregon*
> *c/o Gold Road M &M Co.*
> *Sunday 24th April, 1910*

My Dear'st Evelyn,

    It is useless, my telling you that I'm utterly ashamed of myself for not having answered your most welcome and interesting letter. It has been on my mind constantly for some time. I would leave the mill with my mind thoroughly made up to drop a note at least, to Evelyn Louise, but always something unlooked for would bob up and rebut it. The mill keeps me 12 to 15 hrs. per day, not including being called out at all hrs. of the night when some little thing would go wrong. The night shift is somewhat new at that kind of work. At times it is enough to make a person use a cuss word—of course you know that I wouldn't—ha ha. What can I do to gain your good graces? For I feel sure that I must be blacklisted before now and I know that I deserve it. My only show is by appealing to your sweet and forgiving disposition. I hope that it won't fail me this time—again—ha ha.

Another apology from Harry. *I always fall for his well-written missives. He learned how to write well during his preparatory school education in England.*

> *Everything else in general is very much as per usual, though I may say duller as there is no great extent of work being done in this section. The mines, or more correctly speaking, prospectors, are only working very small crews. They have been laying several off at the wedge (that's this place) and from all appearances seem as though they were going to run as light handed as possible. The mill, I surmise, will probably close down in a week or so to await more developments in the mine.*
>
> *I have not decided yet whether I will stay here or not. It all depends upon how things pan out after the mill shuts down. Last week I had a letter from a friend offering me a job in a mill at Goldfield so it all depends upon circumstances whether or not I stay. I hate to leave old Oregon. It seems like home to me now. So far, I would like to have it be home, though I do not particularly like this section right here. In fact, I have a notion of buying to lease a ranch there. Would you be so kind as to give me a few pointers, Evelyn? The John Day Valley has more attraction for me. With your assistance I'm confident I could beat this mining game.*

I think Harry is dreaming. One would need to strike it rich in the mining game to have enough money to buy a ranch. There are still small pieces of land for homesteading, but how could one get enough together to make a living from it? Evelyn really did think about the things Harry talked of in his infrequent letters. That was the corker: infrequent. Harry wrote a good letter when he got around to it. His formal education in England shone through his sentences. His words were a pleasure to read, especially for Evelyn, a 29-year-old woman who spent many evenings on their ranch, at home with her father.

By the way, did you ever get that picture of yourself taken? I have often wondered if you had and also if yours truly would ever get one. You have no idea how I would prize it. I would set it upon the mirror stand so that when I looked in the mirror I would see you.

I'll bet he would, probably next to his other best girls. Evelyn believed no man over thirty had been sitting around waiting for a cute little Evelyn unless she was attached to a successful ranch. Her pa was certainly known as a successful landowner. He had been ranching since 1864 when he first homesteaded in the John Day Valley. Now at 75, he was slowing down. His boys were all settled with their own properties now, so Evelyn would get the home ranch as her part of an inheritance. She supposed Harry had figured this out while they dated and enjoyed each other's company.

I wish to thank you for the nice remembrance at Easter and also your kind wishes. It never dawned upon me that Easter was anywhere until I got your post card, every day being alike up in this neck of the woods. It was very thoughtful of you to send me the "Liars" or county newspapers. I did appreciate them immensely. It was just like old times, reading the local items, especially everybody's doings as recorded. You mention stealing eggs on an Easter Sunday. I had quite forgotten that such things existed. Ha Ha. It is so long since I had seen or heard of them.

Humph! Short memory! He is turning my attempt to write an entertaining letter into a plea for sympathy of his mining plight.

Our boarding house is simply a fright. Scrap bacon, coffee that is re-boiled instead of renewed, for breakfast. Mulligan stew, rice and prunes for lunch and dinner is our menu, day in and day out. You can form an opinion how very appetizing and tasty it is.

We are having rather cold and miserable weather here these last few days. It threatens rain but is still holding off. In fact, I think it is too cold for rain — more like snow. You have been mighty goody-goody this winter to have stayed at home so closely, pretty much like myself. I have been only once down to Galice since last August. Now that the nice warm weather is here, or ought to be, I hope you will get around more and enjoy yourself to your little, I may say big heart's content.

Now as it is nearly 11 o'clock, I must quit this scribbling and retire. Glad to hear of your feeling so good, hoping to hear from you soon.

Yours very sincerely,
Harry

Evelyn refolded the letter into her apron pocket. It was time to start Pa's dinner. She would add the letter to the little red box up in her room. The box was just the right size for folded correspondence as it had originally held note cards. The box top sported a picture of two horses running in tandem, most fitting for letters being saved by this rancher's daughter.

CHAPTER TWO

The next morning Evelyn glanced in the mirror before going downstairs. She stopped to study the countenance staring back at her just long enough to be reminded that she was twenty-nine years old, a woman, not the slip of a girl she had been when her mother died and left her to become Pa's housekeeper. Her brothers and sisters had left home and established their own households by 1899, the year Ma passed. As her hand brushed across the family album that occupied the corner of her dresser, she remembered the turn of the century, a dramatic time in her young life. She thumbed through the pages filled with portraits. Her stepbrothers, J.J. and Lincoln, lived in Idaho. Step sister Amy had married at age 15. Les and his wife Martha lived on the Doud place just across the river. Lee and Missy were on a homestead just east of the Collins place. George and Alice were married in 1897 and were busy expanding their house just up the lane from the home place. Pa had helped his sons acquire property nearby, except for Ed who had left home without a word. Her sister Mary lived in town with her husband Mr. Bly. Memories: Evelyn, the baby of the family, had remained on the home place. *Humph! I am a twenty-nine year old baby!* she thought. She closed the album with a snap and headed downstairs to fix breakfast. Pa would be waiting as usual before going out to the barn.

For the past five years she had fixed meals for Pa, kept house, fed chickens, tended the garden, and done the chores of a ranch hand. *Pa relies on me to pay the hired hands and keep ranch records. Spinsters make good bookkeepers. There's the rub. The other day I heard George telling Lee that if I didn't hurry-up, I would be just another old maid,* Evelyn muttered to herself.

Determined to avoid that title, Evelyn was planning another trip to Portland with her favorite chum, Daisy. Flamboyant hats and a carefree spirit made Daisy a perfect traveling companion. These two gals could dance and flirt a bit in Prairie City, but when they arrived in Portland, three hundred miles from home, the fun began. They shopped, played cards, went to shows, sampled the cuisine at fine eateries and put themselves in line to be courted about by the gentlemen of the day. They always had a proper room because Evelyn's pa owned a part of the Imperial Hotel. Looking out for his interests provided a good excuse for the trip. Evelyn gave an excited little sigh just thinking about it as she got to the bottom of the stairs, lighter on her feet than usual.

On their trips from Prairie City, Daisy and Evelyn were not loose women. They carefully perused the men who invited them to dance and dine. Dandies did not interest them, but miners, cowboys, railroaders and businessmen were promising companions. Evelyn had met Harry Smithworth at an earlier time in Portland. Conversation was easy and entertaining as they shared fresh crab at Jake's Crawfish. His adventures through the gold fields of the West fascinated her as much as her ranch life and love of the land intrigued him. Harry and Evelyn seemed to be taking up where they had left off about the time she finished business school.

Unencumbered by permanent employment, he brought his pack horse and rode to Prairie City in November of '08 to work the petered-out Dixie Mine. No miner worth his salt could make a living at Dixie, but the camp was still in operation with many miners trying. Single men as well as some families with children lived at the camp. Paths between tents and buildings were dug in the snow, the sides so deep that little kids thought they were trudging through tunnels to get to the outhouses. The winter weather in 1909 slowed up the mining, but it gave Harry and Evelyn time for ice skating on the pond in the south pasture and sleigh rides in the hack with its rusty runners behind Pa's best team. Afterward they would share hot cocoa with Daisy and her current beau.

Harry's finances dwindled through the frigid work of winter mining. In the summer of 1909 he left Prairie City and headed to southern Oregon where the mines promised to be better. His last letter talked of another winter of mining, again not very pleasant.

Evelyn was now courted by mail. She spent many evenings composing missives of her activities and events that she thought would amuse him. Tales of hikes to the hills in the spring to find a first butter cup, or yellow bells and bird bills, filled one paragraph. A walk by the river in search of watercress filled another. The humor of her violin lessons from Mr. Graves who came from Baker City once a month to instruct the people who had purchased instruments from him was told with cleverness, but it was usually several months before she received a reply.

CHAPTER THREE

Galice, Oregon
1st Aug. 1910

My Dear'st Evelyn,

Here I am on the eve of my departure writing a little note to my best girl. I have had you on my mind for a long time and had the best of intentions, but have not had a chance to write you. I have been back up in the mountains working. I have been up there ever since the latter part of May. However, we have gotten all the work completed, also took out 31 sacks of ore. Last week I came down here to the wedge and have run it through the mill. It turned out fairly good, getting a little bar of gold, a shade over 2 oz. So now I am ready for work again.

The G. R. Coy made me a proposition to take the mill and Cyanide End here, but the salary was not satisfactory. So I have decided to travel. Where I shall hit for is a quandary, most likely South, tho I would love to take a ride on the Sumpter Valley Railroad to see how it is to ride into Prairie City. Then again I might possibly have the good fortune of seeing you. Ha. I will go to Portland first

*to attend to a little business, then probably take the boat to
San Francisco; wish you were going, Louise.*

*Imagine taking a boat trip from Portland to San Francisco
with Harry. It is a pie in the sky idea. He knows it would never
happen so it's easy for him to make the suggestion. I would be
seasick, no doubt about it. I guess I should be pleased that he even
suggests such an outing.*

*The last time Daisy and I were in Portland we did have a bit of
adventure. My friend Richard was addressing the lawyer's con-
vention in the ballroom of the Multnomah Hotel. Lawyers from
around Oregon, Washington, and even California were gathered
to honor Judge Wadell who was retiring from the Oregon Supreme
Court. He was a rather well loved judge, if there could be such a
thing. The food was served exquisitely, champagne was served for
toasting, but the best part was the program after dinner when all
the guests gave the judge a "roasting." Daisy and I, as guests of
Richard, were seated at the head table and could hardly ignore the
opportunity to get in on the Roast. We made up a goofy little poem
since we really didn't know Judge Wadell. Richard whispered to
me that he was married and liked to fish. With that bit of information we stood together and recited:*

*Judge Wadell, you've had a good life
Judge Wadell, you've cherished your wife.
Judge Wadell, you've held one wish
That you could catch a really big fish!*

*It was a bit of nonsense that broke the stuffiness of the occasion
and the Roast continued in grand form. Daisy and I were treated
as heroines of the evening. At least this gives me something to
write to Harry about.*

I am glad to hear that you take an outing occasionally, tho it is not right that you should vent your displeasure on your absent friends. Perhaps it is not altogether their fault. I wish that I could have slipped around by your side while you were doing the roasting stunt. My sentiments would have been that it was not so bad after all. Possibly yours would have been that it's worse. Ha Ha.

It is too bad you won't be in Portland this week. Nothing could give me greater pleasure than to have your company and go sightseeing and take in the plays. I am sure I'll feel lonely. You see the last time I was there, there was always a chance of running across you. This time I'll have nothing to look forward to, poor me! By the way, I would be mighty tickled indeed to have a picture. That one you mentioned will be great for the present. Is it a sweet 17? Pretty close, is it not? Ha ha. I would love to see it, so will thank you in anticipation. Now, please don't disappoint yours truly. You will have to excuse this sawed off letter as this is all the paper I have, my suitcase having gone to Galice today. With my very kindest wishes and hoping you are feeling fine and dandy.

Yours very sincerely,
Harry

P.S. Tell your bald headed music teacher hello for me and for him not to be so severe with his pupil. Please write soon for your letters are most welcome.

Evelyn thought she just might tell her violin instructor to ease up a bit, but she knew she would not point out his lack of hair. He came to Prairie City once a month to give music lessons to the culturally-starved community. Some pupils were children, but others were adults, like Evelyn, who played in the Prairie City orchestra. Occasionally some of the members played in church. Evelyn never played solos as she believed one mistake on the violin would produce an ear-jangling squeak that would jar the joy of Sunday worship. She had decided to give up lessons before she turned 30. Hopefully her life would be taking another direction by then, maybe even marriage and children?

CHAPTER FOUR

Today is August 10 and the Martins have just finished haying. The crew are eager to get to town and visit the pool hall. Pa discourages drinking on his place. Evelyn knew why. His two brothers had been drinkers, one even known as the town drunk. Evelyn's mother and father were pillars of the Methodist church and celebrated with potluck picnics and cider parties at Halloween. A little eggnog at Christmas was the extent of their partying. But even Pa understood the haying crew and their desires. Sweltering men pressed hard to complete the job of raking, bucking, stacking hay and caring for the equipment and animals that made it all happen. All sighed with a huge relief when they beat an impending thunder storm.

Evelyn smiled as the crew headed to town. Her hay fever abated and she set to her delayed task of writing to Harry. She shared the remnants of the summer work, tidy stacks of timothy in every field, except the alfalfa patch, which had been cut and stacked earlier. With luck they would get another cutting there. The results of their garden, peas earlier, green beans and corn were now providing delicious meals as well as food for canning. The work of it pleased her, as soon the shelves would be filled with her jars of pickles, jams, vegetables and fruit. Harry always seemed to like hearing about the ranch, as he fancied he would one day become a rancher instead of a miner, or so he purported in his letters.

Evelyn finished the letter to Harry and prepared it for mailing. Tomorrow she would drive to town in the Model T Ford Pa had purchased. She would call Daisy and set up a time to meet. The end of haying meant a day off for her, too. A dance at the Grange Hall was scheduled for Saturday. Evelyn and Daisy planned to attend.

In the old days, they called it the Harvest Dance, but in 1910 the world was changing, even in the small Eastern Oregon town of Prairie City. Music included jazzy tunes that required faster steps. The traditional waltz was still included in the repertoire, but the younger attendees took their breaks during slow music. Sig Durham clanked the keys of the upright piano to create any tune he chose. Marty Gilstrap kept the beat on his drum set. Jake Smart played the fiddle and the base, whichever he felt like, and the Grange Hall fairly rocked with the noise. Evelyn's bald-headed violin teacher was not included in the group of dance musicians who left their classical training at the door. Chairs ringed the dance floor. Women sat and visited with their neighbors. Most of the men stood around and talked but soon began asking the ladies to dance. Married couples filled a third of the floor, husbands and wives who occasionally changed partners with their friends. Single men and women partnered up, then the women were returned to their seats around the room. Food provided by the Grange ladies enticed the crowd between dances. Sometimes the men carried small bottles of booze, usually leading to trouble. Disagreements caused a settling up with fists outside the hall. Luckily most folks left their guns at home.

Daisy and Evelyn knew nearly everyone at the dance, except for a few cowpokes who had hired on for haying jobs and had yet to move on. They danced with their many acquaintances, young and old. Evelyn had done some dancing in Portland which kept her up on what was new, but she would soon be 30 years old. She wondered if that would put her in a new category. In her mother's day the fate of being unmarried triggered gossip and pity. Today a woman could hold a respectable place in society, but the term of "old maid" often crept into the conversation. Evelyn felt like a fence rider, holding space between two worlds.

After the dance, the gals walked to Daisy's where George and Alice planned to meet them and give Evelyn a ride back to the ranch. "Daisy, are you worried about ever getting married?"

"I admit it crosses my mind, but I still have a good time being single. I guess I could have a good time being married, also," replied Daisy.

"I have too much time to think," said Evelyn. "I don't want to be a lonely woman on the ranch. And then I would love to have children. If I ever had a little boy, I would name him Eddie after my brother. Do you remember Eddie?"

"Everyone remembers your brother who left town after having that awful fight with the school teacher. I remember the story more than your brother, I have to admit."

"Our whole family were victims of gossip, as I recall. Finally the story died down, but we never heard from Eddie again. He was my favorite big brother. The whole thing left a hole in my heart. Anyway, if I ever get married and have a son, I will name him Eddie," repeated Evelyn.

"Just remember, your husband may have something to say about it. Do you have one picked out—husband, I mean?" teased Daisy.

"After dancing with available suitors tonight, I think Harry, the letter writer, might be my best prospect," sighed Evelyn as she saw George and Alice coming to get her.

CHAPTER FIVE

In October, at the end of apple picking season, another letter from Harry brought Evelyn up to date on his activities. It was quite a fine letter written on quality stationery and monogrammed with an "S" for Smithworth, his last name.

In September, a book had come for Evelyn. Harry had mailed Zane Gray's popular book, *The Last of the Plainsmen* with a note that said, "A gift for you. I found it very enjoyable reading and hope you will, too."

> *The Braun Corporation*
> *36371-71 New High Street*
> *Los Angeles, Cal*
> *20 Oct. 1910, 11:15 PM*

My Dear'st Evelyn,

I am really ashamed of myself for not having answered your welcome letter before now. But, my plans have been so uncertain. I thought I would wait until I knew definitely what I was going to do—also where I would be located. Even yet, I do not know for sure, but I felt that I must write a few lines to say hello anyway. I have had a very nice time since leaving Oregon. My stay in Berkeley with Herb Junk was great fun. Fancy me, visiting there for about six weeks — very extravagant indeed for me. He is in the real estate business and doing well so during the day we had our usual rides around the town. He had as many as eight houses being built at a time and, as he supervises all the work himself from the plans to the completion of the house, it keeps him on the jump. In the evenings we would either go to a show, dance, or card party. So you can imagine we had a strenuous time.

I came down to Los Angeles about a month ago. My intentions were to stay 2 or 3 days and call upon a friend, a Mr. Hartley. He is secretary and stockholder in the Braun Corp. Instead of my getting away when I intended, he was anxious for me to stay a few weeks and help them out as they were crowded beyond the limit with school laboratory orders. So here I am yet, but will be able to get away this week having gotten them pretty well cleaned out.

I will move on to Arizona next week some time. I have been working from 7:30 AM 'till 10 and 11 o'clock at night so have not had much time to see all that there is to see here. I want to visit the Catalina plants, take in the glass bottomed boat, etc., before I leave. I wish you were here to go with me. I feel sure you would enjoy the beaches — Venice and Ocean Park are great — all sorts of amusement, open air concerts, etc.

I have spent every Sunday down at Ocean Park with the Hartleys. We would go down Saturday night in the auto and come back Monday morning. Though he traveled back and forward every morning and night, I was content with the weekend trip during the week. You see they are a young couple and you know how that is, Ha Ha.

I am pleased to hear that you and Daisy had such a swell time in the Wallowa Mountains. Personally, I was never over in that section of the country and am sorry now that I did not take a trip over there. So many have talked very highly of it, especially the fishing.

By the way, I was almost afraid that you had already read that story I sent you. I am glad it was a book you had not read before and that you enjoyed it.

When I left Southern Oregon the fire was taking a wide swath of timber on the opposite side of the river. In fact, on our way to Merlin from Galice we crossed the river at the ferry and passed through the edge of the fire about half way to town. Quite a lot of homesteaders had lost everything except their cabins, those being saved by having ploughed land around. It certainly has done lots of damage and caused no end of hardships.

I am looking forward very anxiously for your professionally photographed picture, Louise, and will most assuredly let you know right off the reel when I get located. Thanks for the snap shot. The operator was a little too far off to make your faces very distinct.

I am beginning to nod, so will quit, hoping you are fine and dandy and that I will have the pleasure of hearing again from you soon. The enclosed address will find me alright. Many thanks for your very kind wishes. I am most sincerely yours,

Harry

CHAPTER SIX

Well, that explains it! Evelyn fumed under her breath. Two months waiting for a reply to her end-of-summer letter made her a bit testy when she thought about Harry. Traipsing around the country made him interesting, but not very reliable as a beau. *I'll write him when I get good and ready,* she muttered to herself. Next she prepared to drive the Ford to Prairie to share parts of the letter with Daisy. Her father always raised an eyebrow on his bearded face when a letter came from Harry. He considered him a "fly by nighter," even though he seemed well-spoken and educated. Evelyn sometimes even concealed the mail so Pa couldn't see when a letter came. He also raised his eyebrow when no mail came. Evelyn felt she just couldn't win. But her good manners did encourage her to reply.

She put together a little package with her picture as she had promised Harry and sent it to his new address. She was never totally satisfied with photographs of herself, but had delayed far too long in sending this one. After all, she wanted there to be no excuse for Harry to forget her. They had some rocking good times when he was last here. She was ready to repeat them again, when another missive from Harry arrived in the mail.

True to his word, Harry wrote from the mine in Oatman, Arizona.

> c/o Tom Reed Mine
> Oatman, Arizona
> 9th Jan., 1911

My Dear'st Evelyn,

You must think me a very ungrateful piece of humanity for not having answered your most welcome letter ere this. To tell the truth, I have started to write several times but always got interrupted through some cause or other. Last night while at work (graveyard shift) my thoughts were away back in the John Day country "which is not unusual." Then and there, I made a resolution to write you today sure. So here I am, trying to fulfill the promise I made myself.

First of all, I wish to thank you very, very much indeed for your photo and kind wishes. I think that it is very good. The expression is elegant. Words will not suffice to tell you how much I prize it. I have put it on a little bracket where I can always take a peek at you. You look sweeter than ever, Louise, it is too bad it had the misfortune to get split in the mail. It is checked clear down through your left eye, also the corner of your mouth. However, that cannot lessen my admiration.

How did you spend Christmas? I do hope you had a nice time and much better & jollier than you had anticipated. Had I been nearer, nothing would have pleased me more than to have had the honor to call around and wish you the season's greetings, also taken that sleigh ride. Gee, but that would have been mighty fine. It is just my luck. Sometime I hope it may be realized. Did you go sleighing?

Personally I had a quiet time Xmas. Sleeping during the day and work after 11:00 P.M. though everybody had a dandy time Xmas Eve. They had a Xmas tree. The kiddies gave an entertainment which was really good after which the presents were distributed. What do you think! I got a red silk stocking full of chocolates, also a nice white handkerchief. It was quite a surprise, being practically a stranger in the camp. I expected to get nothing. They also had a dance afterward. On New Year's Eve they had a masquerade dance which was a swell affair. There were crowds from Gold Roads and Kingman. Autos were very much in evidence.

So you could not locate Oatman, Evelyn. I don't blame you for I do not think it is on the map, but to give you an idea, it is about 25 miles from the Needles, Calif. on the Ariz. side of the Colorado River and about the same distance from Kingman, Ariz. and four miles from Gold Roads. It is practically a new camp, been working about 2 years. Tom Reed Mine is a very rich property, as good if not better than the Goldfield Consol at Goldfield. They flew last month's clear up from only ten stamps which was $60,000 to this month which will be about $80,000. It is enormous. Yes! I am still at the mining as you surmise, but have wiggled out of the hard and strenuous underground work. Am in the Cyanide plant here. It is more interesting, clean, easy work and much better pay. I consider myself lucky in getting on here, for I never saw so many idle men as there are in this section of the country. They flock in here for the winter from the cold climate. Fortunately for me, there are very few cyanide men.

I had a nice time last summer after leaving Galice last August—went to Portland first, stopping there 5 days.

From there I came on to San Francisco, Oakland and Berkeley where I stayed until the beginning of Oct.—partly on pleasure and business. From there I came on to Los Angeles to visit a friend, T. A. Hartley, secretary and part owner of the Braun Corp., a mine and assay supply Co. I only intended to stay a few days and pulling out, but he finally pressured me to go to work and help them over the busy season, which I did.

I had a swell time. He and his young wife were living down at Ocean Park so we travelled back and forth in the machine, occasionally, as I did not like to impose too much upon good nature. You know there are moments when a young couple likes to be alone, so I'd excused myself as much as the law would allow.

Have you been down around the Los Angeles country, Evelyn? It is surely great, continuous summer. Then again the seaside resorts are fine. By the way, I was almost positive that I saw Jack Galbraith one day in L.A. in a street car uniform. I was talking to a gentleman in the Hollenbeck Hotel at the time or would have hailed him and made sure. I kept a look out after that, but never saw him again. If it was him, he was looking fine, better than I ever saw him. I must keep an eye open for him the next time I'm in L.A.

I suppose Prairie City is quite proud of itself now that the railway is there. Have they gotten the depot finished? How does it compare with the one at Austin? Ha ha, more elaborate I guess. To keep up this scribble only means to bore you the more, so will quit and get ready for work. I have always known and said that you were a good natured and kind-dispositioned girl. Glad you have owned up to it at last. I hope that you will show it again by writing soon.

Again, thanking you for the photo though I would much rather have done it verbally. You are too far away. My arms are not long enough. Ha ha.

> *Yours very sincerely,*
> *Harry*

P.S. Forgive me if I already told you about my visit in Los Angeles. I may have forgotten what I wrote in last year's letter.

CHAPTER SEVEN

He sure did forget! A lot of ranching passes between his letters. Feeding cattle in winter from last summer's stacks of hay was tiresome, cold work. New grass in the meadow meant an end to hitching the team to the wagon and visiting the stack being used for feed, wielding the pitchforks full on the wagon and then off again as the team slowly circles the pasture with the cows trailing behind.

A good crop of calves survived their winter births. Only twice had Pa and the hired hand brought new babies into the kitchen to be warmed by the stove to get their circulation going so they could huddle next to their moms outside or in the barn to nurse. One calf was born breech and did not survive. Evelyn always hated to see the wild-eyed state of a cow which had lost her offspring.

As usual, spring arrived and after a couple of months grazing the meadows near the river, the cattle were moved to the hill pastures where green grass could be found, a result of the melting of the snows and the spring rains. This was a short drive, not much more than opening the gates to the hill pastures. It was good to get the stock out of the meadows so hay could grow. The calves with their new brands on the left hips followed their mothers with their tails arched at the rump and actually frolicked along.

Irrigating began in earnest as rains stopped. Dams with head gates were repaired in the river and the hired hand was sent out with his shovel to direct ditches of water into the grass that would soon grow into hay. The yearling steers rated a pasture of their own as they were the next crop of grass-fed beef to be shipped out in the fall.

Evelyn had made little gifts for her nieces and nephews at Christmas time and went with Daisy to Portland in February. She found herself sighing more than she had the year before. When she lay in bed in the upstairs room, she would think of the year of 1911 as "the year of sighs." She heaved a sigh over bad weather, muddy roads, ranch bookkeeping, and just about anything else that came up. One might call it a "spinster syndrome." The letters to and from Harry had been far and few between and Evelyn's heart had not been into writing and encouraging this long-distance friendship, which some might call a romance.

CHAPTER EIGHT

Oatman, Arizona
c/o Tom Reed Mine
Sunday Eve, 15 Oct. 1911

My Dear Evelyn,

I have been waiting patiently for ages for some news of you, but alas, none is forthcoming. So I have decided not to endure the suspense any longer, hence this note of investigation. Of all things I do hope you are well, also your good friend Daisy. Is she still down in Canyon City? The summer in camp has been very quiet indeed, which I attribute to the absence of the ladies who have all been to the coast during the hot summer months. Now that they are all back again, I surmise that things will take on their usual appearance. They have had two dances which were very enjoyable. They also have a moving picture show every Friday night. How is that for a mining camp! The company put up a swell hall to be used for dancing and shows—stage at one end—reading room and cloak room at the other. They installed a new piano a short while ago. There are also several musicians in camp so the dances are well supplied with music.

Say, Louise, I thought I should have died this summer. The heat was something fierce. The mercury stood around 118 degrees in the shade. The water which is piped for several miles into camp was absolutely red hot. A person had to let it stand overnight in order to let it get cool enough to wash in and to drink. The most trying of all was the sleeping when working night shifts and having to sleep during the day time. I had all four sides of my tent up. Then with a tub of cold water close by I would take a duck and lay down on top of the bed without drying myself. What little air there would be would feel quite cooling when it struck the moisture. After 2 or 3 ducks I would eventually fall asleep only to wake up in a pool of perspiration. I also had a wet canvas stretched over the bed about 2 ft. high. I am mighty glad to see this cool weather come again. Though, during the day it is still hot, but the nights are swell.

I surmise that Prairie City has trebeled itself since the railroad got there. I'm afraid I would be unable to find my way around the burg now. How is the street car business, Lou? I'd be a complete stranger there now. Would you be condescending enough to show yours truly the sights should I ever be fortunate enough to visit the City?

Am on graveyard shift so must go. Trusting you are fine and dandy.

Yours very sincerely,
Harry

P.S. Please drop a line at your leisure, Louise. Tell Daisy hello for me. Adieu, in haste.

Harry pleads a sad case for his hard work and gruesome weather. He seems truly interested in me and the other people he met in P.C. I could do worse than this educated man from England. He knows mining. He knows travel. He does know me, but does he love me? Why else would he keep writing even when I don't answer?

CHAPTER NINE

The ranch. Evelyn returned to her pondering again. *He wants to own land. Does he see me as a way to inherit this valuable piece of ranch land? Ma is gone. Pa is old. My brothers and sister are "fixed." When Pa goes, I will be left with this property, unless I marry and move away first.*

Would I marry Harry if he asked me and move to a hot or cold mining camp? Would I be willing to leave this home I've always known? It's been my household for 15 years. If I sit here as an old maid, who will I get to run the place?

Full of doubts, Evelyn sat at her mother's secretary to compose yet another letter to Harry.

Prairie City, Oregon
Saturday, 21 Oct. '11

Dear Harry,

Typical of October, the leaves on our orchard trees have changed color, dried to crinkles and blown to the ground. Plans for the Halloween social at the Grange Hall are underway. As usual, Daisy is in charge of setting up the various booths for crocheted baby garments, quilts, and baked goods. The money raised will buy the food for the Thanksgiving dinner presented by the Grange members. This is about the most excitement we will experience in Prairie City. Our last big celebration was when the train of the Sumpter Valley Railroad chugged into town from Baker City. Frankly, I find life a bit lonely between our few social occasions. I would also enjoy some of your Arizona heat as my car won't warm up until I'm halfway to town.

Did I tell you Pa bought a Model T for our personal use? We drove it up by Lee's place last month when he was trying to drive his sheep up the road to the upper pasture gate. You know how we cattle ranchers dislike those blatting sheep! To make matters worse, the lead ewe got herself caught between the fender and front tire. Lee, in his furry, told us to, "Get that pile of junk off the road!" so we high-tailed it home to keep peace in the family.

My next adventure was when Daisy and I took George and Alice's children to Baker City to the circus . . . I was the old-maid auntie keeping track of all four of them. Actually, it was nice to get everyone home safe and sound with only one little boy lost temporarily.

I hear Bert and Amy Roberts struck it rich over on the Green Horn. Do you ever hear from him? I look forward to hearing more from you about Arizona and the successful Tom Reed Gold Mine. If you ever get back to Oregon, I will show you around the town and the changes that have been made. The truth of the matter is that I am a bit lonesome as the fall weather is upon us.

Sincerely yours,
Evelyn

Evelyn reread the letter to see if the tone suited what she wanted to say: interested but not passionate. She sealed the envelope and stamped it, ready for the next trip to town to the post office.

Box 102
Oatman, Arizona
19th Dec. '11

My Dearest Evelyn,

I have felt like writing to you several times since I received your most welcome letter, but thought that I had better wait a week and wish you the season's greetings to save you the *care * of reading two of my letters so closely following each other. Gee, how I wish that I had control of the elements and could send you some of this beautiful weather for it is certainly great, warm during the day and just cool enough at nights for one to sleep his best. Though, occasionally we do get some terribly cold snaps which usually last about 3 days. Then everyone almost freezes to death as no one is prepared.

You do not half know how sorry I am to hear of you being so lonesome at the ranch—how I would like to have the pleasure of surprising you by dropping around and visiting a while, but to me it seems almost too good to ever materialize. I sure appreciate your very kind offer to take me about the burg. To have everything look its best to me you surely would have to be with me. Your account of the trip to Baker and the circus was rather comical. I can just picture how motherly you would look taking care of the little folks. Possibly something or someone more to your liking, caused you to leave and forget the little boy—he was fine, no harm done. As to you being in the old maid ranks—that is purely nonsense, Louise, I hope that you never will, but probably you have gotten that all figured out to your own satisfaction.

No, I have never had a scratch from Bert Roberts since he left Portland. I do not know his address, though, I am mighty glad to learn of his prosperity. They both deserve to get along well.

The dances have started again. They hold two every month and have a swell time, though, I rarely go as it is a case of going alone. They had a basket social a short while ago for the benefit of the school kiddies' Christmas presentation. So, I guess that will be the next big doing. The social netted over $300.00 which I thought was fairly good for the camp.

Fortune in the way of dinners have been coming my way great lately. I was out to a turkey feed at the MacLear's on Thanksgiving Day and have had several chicken ones since then and have an invite out to another turkey dinner Xmas. By that time I ought to be in pretty good condition myself.

Now, Louise, I guess I have got to quit. I have a miserable dull cyanide headache tonight and can think of nothing interesting. So again wishing you a very merry and happy Christmas and may the New Year bring all your little heart's desires. Hoping you are fine and dandy and that I'll hear from you soon.

> Very sincerely yours
> Harry

P.S. Tell Daisy hello. Trusting she will have a good time Xmas, also.

CHAPTER TEN

Harry gets sentimental and lovey-dovey around the holidays. No one hears much when it's cold and miserable in our part of the country. He's nice and warm in Arizona. I'm too busy to think about him right now! Evelyn muttered to herself.

The family Christmas celebrations were upon the Martins. They would go to George's for dinner and share gifts. The wrapping of Evelyn's gifts for the children would occupy most of the day. Pa would ask the family to go to church on the Sunday before Christmas

Christmas Eve would be special for the children. Each would receive a gift from the family and then the extra ones that Aunt Evelyn had wrapped in special red paper and tied with fancy bows. Evelyn always imagined how it would be to wrap special gifts for a child of her own. She even pictured in her dreams what a little girl or boy would look like if Harry were the father. *I wonder if he wants to become a parent,* she muttered to herself. The subject of what comes after a couple gets together to start a family had never come up between them. Harry rarely got beyond thinking what life would be like as a rancher rather than a miner.

Oh pshaw! I'm thinking like a 15 year old girl who dreams, rather than a 30 year old woman who knows what life is really like. Come to think of it, my mother was 29 when she married Pa.

The only difference is that she already had three children from a first marriage.

Marriage may not be what it is cracked up to be. I know for sure the hard work never ends, and it must take just the right husband to make it pleasurable. Once one is married, the world knows the woman was desirable to someone!

Too bad Harry isn't here because Pa and George will put sled runners on the old hack, hitch up the team and take everyone for a sleigh ride, wrapped in blankets and listening to the bells that are put on the harness during the holidays. But, he is enjoying the warm weather in Arizona, eating turkey dinner with some mining family," Evelyn thought.

CHAPTER ELEVEN

Evelyn called Daisy, thinking what a joy it was to have a telephone, even if there were a number of people on the party line and they could hear one's conversation by just picking up the receiver from the oak box that hung on the kitchen wall. All the people know the rings of the other people on the line, and those rings came into the house every time there was a call. At least the phone saved a trip to town just to talk something over.

"Daisy, how would you like to go to Portland for a few days? The weather is not too bad. We could take the train to Baker City and then on down to Portland. If you want to go, I will write the Imperial for reservations; my treat. Pa needs someone to look over the books down there so I could do that while we are there." Evelyn was pretty sure Daisy would accept.

"Evelyn, you read my mind! I am dying to get out of Prairie for a few days. My hat business is at a standstill. Everyone has a winter hat to keep her head warm and fashions for spring are not yet on anyone's mind. I could locate a few little numbers to bring home for Easter so my little shop will be prepared when the Ladies' Aid meets in April for their big 'do,' raising money for orphans."

Evelyn listened to Daisy as she had many times before. Daisy thought the money should be spent here in Prairie instead of being sent to the African orphans, but the church board had made up its mind to help out the Methodist missionaries.

Europe was in a mess, according to the newspapers, and the women in Oregon still did not have the vote. Evelyn remembered how her mother would have felt about that. Anyway it seemed like a good time to get away from the ranch routine. Sometimes ranching was not all it was cracked up to be. Maybe Harry should think about that.

CHAPTER TWELVE

Oatman, Arizona
c/o Tom Reed Mines
6/23/12

My Dear Evelyn,

Neglect? Well it is a way yonder worse than that!
Absolute desertion I call it. Possibly you have called it
much worse than that, which I confess would be the correct
name, whatever it was. It isn't because I haven't thought of
you for I very, very often picture you in my mind's eye and
think how sweet you are. I'm afraid to tell all in case I get
roasted when you write. It is more on account of the climate.
A person feels languid and dopy night and day, don't feel
like doing a thing. The heat is fierce. I was also gone about
2 months on a trip through Nevada and California and So.
Oregon. I went to look over the tailing dumps at the various
camps with the view of leasing, but did not find anything
worthwhile. So I returned to the Tom Reed again and work.
I visited Goldfield, Tonopah, Silver Peak, Manhattan, Elk
Nevada, Grass Valley, Nevada City and several others in
Calif. and went as far as my property in Southern Oregon.
Gee, how I would have liked to have kept going until I

reached the John Day Valley, but I overstayed my leave of absence so had to hike back with all haste, stopping off at San Francisco and Los Angeles. I was also fortunate to be in Sacramento during the aviation meet. It was mighty fine, tho it could have been greatly improved with you being there with me. I did not meet a soul I knew so was mighty lonesome. I left there that very night.

The Sunday Oregonian just arrived tonight giving a glowing account of their festival and Rose Carnival. I wondered if you were there in the maddening throng. Should have liked to have been there myself. How are all the Prairieites, nothing startling I suppose, tho one never can tell as there is always a chance for an elopement or something sensational in the lively berg, which it no doubt is now that the Mormon Railroad runs into it.

By the way, Evelyn, do you want a haying hand this summer? If so, I do hereby apply for the job. It would do me good to get where there are trees and vegetation again, especially when you were there too. Since I came back I got promoted a notch, to the zinc room, taking care of the cyanoid solutions, melting bullion, etc. I like it fine, not so very much to do, clean work. Last month's cleanup was a little over $90,000. It is never below $70,000 per month. I am going to try for another step, that of the assay office in a week or so. The money is the same, but a fellow gets lots of outside assaying to do, which is all velvet, making it a better money job in the long run. Whether I will get it or not remains to be seen.

A short while ago we had quite an excitable time here in camp, two shooting scrapes in one week. One fellow got shot in the mouth, for which the other guy is doing time. The other passed off without any bloodshed. About 4 days ago a boy got bitten with a rattlesnake. They dressed it with permanganate, filled the kid up with whiskey. He is now about well again. Thanks to the whiskey, I guess. Ha Ha.

After I change shifts I intend taking a few snap shots of the camp if you care to have a few views of Arizona as it is at Oatman. I would be only too pleased to send them. Now I must not tire you out reading so will stop this scribble and retire.

Say, Louise, please do not try to get even with me by delaying your letter. I would like very much to hear from you soon to learn how you are. I hope I have half way explained my seeming neglect. What I would really like to say is that I think we would make a wonderful couple. I am thinking in a permanent sort of way. Please respond with your thoughts. With my very kindest wishes, hoping you are fine and dandy and free from hay fever. Is this about the time you get it? Ever yours most sincerely,

Harry

P.S. Tell Daisy hello.

Was that a proposal? 'We would make a fine couple.' Is this letter the same as Harry down on one knee popping the question, or is he still just feeling the water? A sigh of exasperation escaped Evelyn's lips as she finished the letter.

I plan to make things happen in my life! Ridges of determination creased her forehead, as Evelyn talked out loud to herself. I do not need a husband to be a successful ranch owner. Too many women succumb to the age-old feelings of needing a man!

This letter has it again. Harry always ends his letters by inquiring about Daisy. Maybe he should be writing to her!

Always apologizing for not writing. He'd be here in a minute if he thought he could take over part of this ranch! I sound like a jealous girlfriend. This is stopping now. I am through talking to myself.

She temporarily put Harry and his letters out of her mind. The Ladies Aid Society had enlisted 90% of the women in the valley to collect money and goods to send to the African mission. The picture taken in front of the church had fifty women lined up dressed to the hilt with their best hats tilted and plopped on their heads. One look at the picture made Evelyn realize Daisy was right to bemoan the state of women's hats in Prairie. A trip to Portland is high priority. Daisy needed some exciting merchandise for her little hat shop. *I am just the one to help her out with a buying trip,* Evelyn decided.

CHAPTER THIRTEEN

Evelyn knocked on Daisy's door with her beige-gloved hand. The entrance to Daisy's stood on the back street of Prairie, just up a rocked-in walkway through a small grassy patch and some petunia beds. Daisy's other entrance was the store front where her hats and gloves were displayed. Most prominent on display sat the magenta- and red-feathered concoction she had brought from Portland on her last trip. It reminded Evelyn of the humungous hats Missy Martin used to wear to church. Evelyn liked sitting in the pew behind Missy because it blocked the view of the minister. As a short person, Evelyn could not be seen by the minister or the choir in case she made a face if she didn't like the sermon or the songs. What a peculiar memory to have as she waited for Daisy to come to the door.

"Daisy, let's go to Portland. Pa says I can go ahead and take the Model T. We can spend the first night in Prineville and go on in to the Imperial Hotel for the second night. You can make appointments in the garment district to look at the new hats and gloves. I was just looking at that Ladies' Aid picture and realizing half of those women are ready for new hats."

Before Daisy could answer, Evelyn went on, "I will pay for the room and you can buy me a new fall hat. I saw a picture in the St. Louis catalogue that looked as if a shorty like me could wear it. It was dark blue with white trim, just perfect for my winter coat."

Daisy was determined not to go to market until she sold her feathered creation from the front display. But, Evelyn's enthusiasm weakened her resolve, so the ladies sat down with a cup of tea to make travel plans.

"How many days will you require to go to market?" asked Evelyn.

"I will spend a full day in the chapeau salon. Then back in the hotel we will work up an order, check out prices, and return the next day to arrange to have the goods packed for shipping."

"Do you think we could get them in the back of my car?"

"You know, hats are smaller this year. I'll bet we could bring them home with us," said Daisy. "When will you be through haying?"

"We should finish up the first of August. Let's plan on going August 6," suggested Evelyn.

As the plans were set, Evelyn gave Daisy a sly smile. "Can I try on the feather hat?" she asked.

Daisy complied and lifted the feathery creation to Evelyn's head. The two women looked in the mirror, Evelyn turning her head from side to side. Then, a little giggle escaped her lips, and another, and one from Daisy. Before long the women were laughing with hearty guffaws, holding their sides to keep their ribs from hurting.

"I wonder if Harry would like me in a hat like this," Evelyn pondered.

"Too bad he won't be in Portland so you can ask him. Have you heard from him again?" asked Daisy.

"Yes, I have another letter to discuss with you. It will give us something to talk about on our way to Portland."

The two women dropped the subject of Harry for the time being, and Daisy returned the monstrous hat to its perch in the window.

Evelyn drove home feeling relaxed. Maybe all she had needed to put herself in a good mood after Harry's last letter was a good laugh with her chum, Daisy.

CHAPTER FOURTEEN

The end of June and the first day of summer pushed the Martins to irrigate all day and sometimes into the night. This is when hay must grow. The cattle had been sent to mountain range and the hay was coaxed to grow thick and tall to guarantee winter feed for the herd. Pa hired Clive Jones to help irrigate. He went home at night so Evelyn only cooked extra for the noon meal, the big one they called dinner. When they started haying, it would be another matter. The little bunk house would need a good cleaning to house the hands who came through and hired out to help cut, rake, buck and stack the hay.

Evelyn took the broom covered with an old pillowslip out to the bunk house. From top to bottom she flushed the spiders and crawling critters from their winter homes and laid out sheet blankets for the two beds. The mattresses were probably 40 years old. No one paid attention as it was just an old log cabin that was used for three weeks in the summer and otherwise forgotten. Pa had built it back in the 1860s when he homesteaded the property as a young man. Evelyn's thoughts switched to Harry as she swept and cleaned. She knew mining camps were not fancy, but she doubted this would even suffice if he came to help hay as he had suggested. He wouldn't be coming to work, just to woo her in hopes of becoming a ranch owner one way or the other.

The Martins had a crew put together by the tenth of July, so haying began in earnest. Hot weather was welcome for the hard push to beat any summer rain storms. If raked-up hay got wet and had to be turned over to dry, the job took longer and cost more.

Evelyn served up biscuits and sausage gravy every day at 6:00 a.m. when the men hit the back door after their stops at the outhouse and back porch sink to wash up. The dew on the hay dried while the men ate so they could harness the teams and cross the river bridge, sickle bars standing high and bouncing as the teams stepped out with their mowing machines. Evelyn liked to see them all take off for the morning work. She poured the last cup of coffee and treated herself to a private ten minutes. As usual, Harry crept into her daydreams.

Will Harry be my last chance to marry? she thought. *Will I be like the woman with a dowry — give away the ranch to get the man?* Evelyn shook her head. *Oh for goodness sakes, listen to me. This muttering has to stop!*

She looked up at the sound of hooves on the bridge. Out the back door, she saw Clive struggling to hold an unconscious figure in front of him in his saddle. With a heart-wrenching gasp, Evelyn ran down the steps to help Clive lower the limp body to the ground.

CHAPTER FIFTEEN

Evelyn cradled Pa's head as he lay on the ground. "Clive, ring up Laura. Tell her we are bringing Pa into the hospital. He's hurt bad. Have them get Doc Orting over there right away! Bring a couple of sheet blankets from that cupboard by the fireplace!" Evelyn issued orders like a nurse and drill sergeant rolled into one.

The Prairie City Hospital was established in 1910. It was the prime place to get treatment in the whole of Grant County. *We just need to get him there*, thought Evelyn.

"Laura will get the doc," reported Clive as he rushed from the house with the supplies Evelyn had requested. "Your pa lost his balance and gave a yell when he stepped in a mud hole. It scared John's team and they took off with the mower which clipped your dad's leg. I got him in my saddle and home as fast as I could," explained Clive, who looked as pale as Pa. Evelyn spread the sheet blanket on the ground and helped Clive lift Pa onto it. Then she ripped the other sheet into wide strips and wrapped the damaged leg, attempting to stem the bleeding. Pa began to moan. Evelyn felt joy with every groan as it assured her he was still alive.

"Crank that auto! Let's get my pa to town as fast as we can!" said Evelyn, as a burning bile rose in her throat.

Evelyn was thankful their Model T was a two-seater, four-door model so they could load Pa into the back and head for town. Clive took the "shotgun" seat and Evelyn far surpassed the 20 mile per hour speed limit as they rolled over the three miles to the hospital. Dr. Orting and his nurse took over the medical examination, and Evelyn exhaled her first sigh of relief as she relinquished the responsibility for her father's care to the professionals.

Clive sat for a time with Evelyn in the waiting room, shaking his knees, tapping his boots on the scrubbed wood floor, and looking miserable.

"Clive, could you go find my sister Mary and tell her where I am and then get hold of George? Tell him what happened and ask him to get hold of Lee. I think my brothers and sister who are here would want to know about this accident." Evelyn was beginning to calm down and issue orders again.

After about an hour, Dr. Orting appeared in the waiting room. "Evelyn, I believe in addition to the cuts and scrapes, which we have cleaned up, Thomas has dislocated his left hip. It could have happened when he fell or it could be the cause of the fall. It often happens to people his age. Go on up to his room to let him know you are here before he falls asleep. We will have a more definitive answer about the injuries as soon as he is more comfortable and we can take him to our new x-ray equipment for a picture."

Evelyn climbed the stairs to his room, kissed his cheek and squeezed his uninjured hand before he dozed off. This accident forced her to think about running the ranch with Pa unable to help. The whole family would be concerned about his health, but it is just human nature to think about inheriting land and money when the patriarch of a family passes on. Evelyn shook her head as if to clear the thoughts from her brain. The job of nursing Pa back to health would be next on her agenda.

CHAPTER SIXTEEN

For a man his age, Pa recovered amazingly well. Dr. Orting loaned a wheel chair to the Martins when Evelyn drove him home after a two week hospital stay. He was assigned to bed and wheelchair for another four weeks. Pa was not one to enjoy being pushed about, and he for sure didn't want to hear the common comment that a broken hip was the end of life for most old people. Recovery went so well that Evelyn dismissed her thoughts of Harry and what kind of help he would have been on the ranch if he had been here. Haying was finished the first of August just as planned. Evelyn felt proud as she paid the crew and tallied up the expenses. She would need to find someone to come stay with Pa when she and Daisy made their trip to Portland, but she was deserving of a much-needed change of scenery.

While Pa was in the hospital, Evelyn cooked for the men, then drove the Model T to town to see how her father was recovering. Taking the car every day meant she had to put her strength to the crank to start it. Actually, owning a new car to crank made a fairly easy job of it. She often saw men in their shirt sleeves trying to get their two- and three-year-old cars going again after a stop. Evelyn was no longer worried about driving the Model T to Portland when she and Daisy were ready to head out.

After supper, she would tally the men's hours so their checks could be ready the day haying ended. When she brought Pa home, he was pleased with the way the ranch had been run. "Pa, you know I had been planning that trip to Portland to help Daisy buy her new line of hats before your accident. Now that you are home, haying is complete, and the books are up-to-date, I think we will go ahead and leave next week." Evelyn saw the worry lines on Pa's face deepen as he listened. "George will send his older children over. Cleeta will stay with you to cook and do the house-work. Lyle will come over every day to help with chores. Clive will continue to work for us, get the water back on the fields, repair equipment, get ready to fence the haystacks and so on. Besides, I will only be gone a few days." Evelyn knew the old man sitting before her in the wheelchair did not cotton to her arrangements but would not fight her on it. She was glad to have her plans out in the open. Tomorrow she would reconfirm it all with Daisy. *Maybe I will even dream a bit about Harry tonight.*

CHAPTER SEVENTEEN

With bags packed and a twitter of excitement, the two ladies hit the road. The Martin's Model T was well-cared for and drove like a charm. It had been Pa's one extravagant expense now that his ranch was complete and his children had their own places. Evelyn drove the car to take Pa to church and to show off a bit when she went to the Ladies' Aid meetings.

Once out of town, they opened the windows and let the scarves at their necks blow with abandon. They would put the car into hotel parking once they reached Portland and enjoy shopping strolls and streetcar rides, a novelty for the gals from tiny Prairie City.

"Daisy, I have been waiting to talk about Harry with you. In his last letter he said he thought we might make a good team in a permanent sort of way, and what did I think about that. Before I could do my thinking and pen an answer, Pa was hurt and his recovery and our job of putting up the hay was all I could think about. Do you think his letter was the same as a proposal, or just fishing for information?"

"Evelyn, do you ever think about how long you two have been corresponding?" asked Daisy.

"Of course I do. Harry has always been entertaining. He is well-educated and rises above any man in our town who is a prospect. I want to be married. Knowing that people call me an "old maid" behind my back is hurtful. But there is Pa who needs me to keep the ranch operating. I don't know how much help Harry would be, and I don't want to ride off to some mining camp with him. If I really loved him, would I even care?"

"You are over-thinking the whole thing. Let's just head for a good time in Portland. Maybe we will meet the men of our dreams. I don't want to be an old maid either," said Daisy.

Evelyn put her foot to the accelerator and decided Daisy was right.

Two days later they rolled into Portland right down Broadway and parked at the Imperial Hotel. The bellman took their bags in and made arrangements to park the Model T, promising it would be gassed up and ready to go when their stay was over.

They were escorted to room 612, a corner room over-looking Broadway. They could see the new ice cream parlor looking west and the theater beyond that. Down two blocks to the east and closer to the river was the Multnomah Hotel. They planned to freshen up and make their way to that dining room for dinner.

As they were seated for dinner, Daisy spotted Mo Morton across the room. He came over to their table to greet Daisy and invite her to see his new hat displays at the clothing market. Daisy set a date to see his booth at 11:00 the next morning.

After Mo left their table, Daisy said, "You must come with me tomorrow, Evelyn. Mo always invites me out for the evening, and he will have a friend to join us. Entertaining clients may be on his expense account, but he knows how to show ladies a good time."

In bed that evening, Evelyn sighed as she thought of tomorrow's plans and pushed her thoughts of Harry to the back of her mind.

True to Daisy's promise, Mo's friend Ira Adler was charming and helped Mo show the girls a good time. Dinners out and two trips to the theater satisfied their urge for entertainment. Daisy chose the new fall hats for her shop at home and arranged to have them boxed and delivered to the hotel. On Friday, the gassed up car was brought around and carefully loaded for the trip home.

Evelyn knew as soon as she arrived back at the ranch and saw that Pa was recovering well, she would write to Harry, explain why it had taken such a long time for her reply, and see if he mentioned a permanent "getting together" again. She could put it off no longer. Harry would certainly be a better ranchman than someone like Ira Adler.

CHAPTER EIGHTEEN

Evelyn sent brother George's children home and helped Pa to bed. The trip had refreshed her spirit and the task of caring for her pa was less difficult than when she and Daisy had left. It was a wonderful adventure driving to Portland, feeling so independent and sophisticated, but as she fell into bed, tired as a limp lily, she vowed to take the train next time. After all, everyone was proud of Mr. DeWitt's Sumpter Valley railroad. She would support it with her patronage.

Evelyn rose to her usual chore of putting on the water for the morning oatmeal. Then she went to help Pa into his wheelchair. He reminded Evelyn again that she made wonderful oatmeal, next only to her mother's. Then he relived the day he came to the house and found Ma collapsed on the kitchen floor. Although that had been fifteen years ago, it was fresh in Pa's mind. Evelyn noticed not all memories were as fresh as this one. She hated to admit it, but Pa was failing in some other ways.

"Pa, what would you think of installing a bathroom and electricity? George and I were discussing it the other day. He is going to do it to his house. We could get an electrician and a plumber and share the cost. How I would love to avoid those trips to the outhouse and the routine of dumping chamber pots." Evelyn appealed to her father's sense of doing what was right for his daughter.

"Let's see how much money we have left after we pay the doctor bills for this pesky hip. I know you would enjoy those comforts, but I wouldn't want to go in debt to do it." Pa's reply closed the matter.

The next mail day brought letters from J.J. and Lincoln, asking about Pa's health. The whole family showed concern for the old man. Evelyn could see his energy was diminished, but they did go over the books regularly. She continued to encourage him to consider electricity and plumbing for the old house.

CHAPTER NINETEEN

The time had come. Evelyn sat down to write to Harry. Pa slept every afternoon, so she took advantage of the time. She explained about the accident and her father's condition and shared most of the details of her trip to Portland with Daisy. She told him of her attempts to have electricity and plumbing installed. The telephone and the Model T were wonderful treasures of the age, and Evelyn pressed on with more. She described the summer and the fall crops, the apples nearly ready for picking, and the canned vegetables she had stored for winter. The weather had been far from perfect, and she told Harry all about it.

She did not bring up his suggestion that they might get together permanently. She left it for him to bring up that subject again if he still felt inclined. The date was close to his birthday so she sent best wishes, and the long overdue letter was mailed the next day. Evelyn was again on the waiting end of their correspondence.

CHAPTER TWENTY

Oatman, Arizona
Box 102
Dec. 4, 1912

My Dearest Evelyn,

How very glad I was when I saw your writing again after having waited so patiently for a long time. Your letter was surely the most pleasant thing I have gotten for ages as it seems we both have been home beings for a long time. In fact, I think that the roving spirit has left me for I have not been out of camp for almost a year in fact. I have no inclination to go anywhere except of course if there were a possibility of seeing you. Then I would be happy to go anywhere. You may not believe that, but it is really so. 1915 is a long time to wait as it is most likely I will take the Fair in, too. Apparently you have not been from home much since you were in Portland with Daisy. I enjoyed what little time we spent together and wish that they could be repeated. How I would like to be a little nearer you so that I might have the pleasure of taking you around a little. Of course, with your consent.

Thanks for your kind birthday greeting. It was very thoughtful of you, Louise indeed. I am almost unable to keep track of the years, not having had a birthday in a long time. After much figuring and study I came to the conclusion that I am in the neighborhood of 37. Old enough now to get married Eh! Ha ha. If I could talk a certain girl in the John Day Valley into the same notion, I surely would, too. Gee!

You said Daisy is dating the sheriff and is so smitten she has lost her appetite. Then you said she was eating again and feeling better. From the rest of your letter I think Prairie is getting more citified every year. I surmise that the new hotel etc. must add greatly to the appearance of the burg. I am sorry to hear that you have had such a stressful summer with your father's accident and the unpleasant weather . . . It seems a shame that it couldn't be more evenly dispersed by you having some of our heat and we here in Arizona getting a little of your cold. It has been ideal summer weather all fall although, I expect that may change.

. . . .

I started to write you several days ago at the office but was interrupted once again. I'll try to finish, being in my bachelor den, there is no chance for disturbance.

We will get our usual cold spell; as a rule the cold snaps only last about 4 days and then it warms up again. Yes, I landed the job I was after. I have the assay job now, have a nice office off by itself and a helper. So, I have a rather comfortable position. I like it fine, having a certain amount of work to take care of. When I get through with it, the time is my own. Sometimes I kick off and see a ball game, which of course, is not a league game, but a game between the camps of Oatman and Goldroads, etc. Still there is lots of fun and good laughs at some of the bonehead plays.

The mine still is turning out about the usual amount of gold. Last month's assay returns on the bullion was $133,000. This month which I accepted a few days ago was $120,000. I will enclose a picture if I can find one. It will serve to show you how they ship it. It is in cones instead of bars. The camp is steadily growing and promises to be one of the foremost ere long.

The social clubs have started their dances again — twice a month on the 5th and 20th of each month. They have sell times. The ladies supply the cakes, etc. and are paid for same out of the funds. Coffee is made right in the hall. They have a separate room for same, filled up elegantly with electric percolators, etc. The hours are from 8 to 12 o'clock to allow a fellow a good sleep before going to work. I am somewhat surprised, Louise, to hear of the mining being dead around Prairie. Is the Dixie Meadows closed down too? Whatever became of the rich strikes they made some time ago? I think that it was on Dixie Creek.

Your letter also put me in mind of my acquaintances from Prairie City. Could you bring me up to date on some of them, or has two years been too long to remember what has gone on? I am very sorry indeed to hear that Daisy has been on the sick list. It is surely hard times but, am pleased to note that she is improving, judging from your accounts of her appetite. I guess yes, of course you know, Louise, I don't mean to infer that you have anything other than a dainty appetite yourself. Did she tire of the sheriff's office? By the way, how is friend Charley? I hope fine and dandy. Is Bricktop still to-the-fore as busy as ever, I surmise. He is

a good old scout. And George M., how is he getting along?
I would sure like to see them all again.

Now I must say adieu trusting to all that is fair and holy
that you will not be so long in writing. I look forward to your
letters day by day. They are much appreciated and enjoyed.

> *Yours very sincerely*
> *Harry*

P.S. with my very best wishes, etc., etc.

The Martin family enjoyed the Christmas season of 1912 and renewed their energy for 1913. Pa felt better, but he needed Clive to help with the ranch work. Evelyn felt they would need another hand as spring came on, new calves were born, and fences needed repair. She reread a portion of a letter Harry had written. Somehow the envelope and the first page were lost, but she loved his descriptions of his home in England and his childhood.

Evelyn wished Harry could understand her needs without her having to spell them out. Mining was in his blood, no matter how he professed his desire to be a rancher. She had a wonderful piece of a letter that described his home in England. It sounded to Evelyn like the estate of a gentleman farmer. How could she expect him to come to the ranch as her husband and be bossed around by her, telling him what to do?

Then there was the matter of a family. He was already 37. Would he want children? Could Evelyn have children at 34? Of course her mother birthed her last baby at age 40, but there had been eight born before that. The more Evelyn pondered, the more roadblocks she seemed to throw in the way of a marriage to Harry, even though he had mentioned it again in his last letter

The note on Harry's Christmas card had been most pleasant and Evelyn kept it to reread during the month of January.

I am very much interested in your fiddling. The violin is not only a nice pastime, but a swell thing to be able to handle correctly. That is one thing I've always been sorry for, that is, not having learned to play some musical instrument. I had all the chance a boy needed, but I was just schooled to death and the mention of learning something more gave me pip. That is the reason I know nothing today.

> *Tom Reed Gold Mines Company*
> *PO Box 102*
> *Oatman, Arizona*
> *20th Dec. 1912*

My Dearest Louise,

Just a little note tonight to wish you the season's best greetings. May you have a dandy time Xmas. Say! How I should like to be close by you with a sprig of mistletoe handy. Gee! Ha ha, what would you do to tee a club to me? I wrote you a few days ago, gave most all the news. So this one will be short duration. By the way, I have gotten my wish regarding the weather for it has turned off mighty cold. It froze ice ½ inch thick here last night—something very unusual—causing a rush into the heaviest clothing available. The wind is blowing a hurricane and goes clear through a fellow. There is little satisfaction in being in the house as these rag propositions make mighty feeble efforts to keep the cold out, so it is me for the bed. I do hope that you are not having the cold proportionally. I went to a social dance last night — had a very nice time — but tonight I feel the effects like the sad gray dawn of the morning after which one is far from letter writing form.

So will say adieu again wishing you a very merry Xmas and a happy and prosperous New Year. May you have all your little heart desires. Trusting to hear from you soon.

Yours very sincerely
Harry

P.S. Tell Daisy hello, wishing her the compliments of the season.

CHAPTER TWENTY-ONE

Valentine's Day arrived and the Prairie City residents prepared for the annual box social. Decorations adorned the Grange Hall. Boxes and baskets filled the tables around the perimeter of the hall. Members and guests of the Grange filled the seats in the center to hold the brief business meeting and the auction of the fancy boxes. Money raised from the event would be used to pay for the Baker City veterinarian to make a visit to the county to provide vaccine for ranchers who could not afford to vaccinate their herds on their own

As usual Evelyn and Daisy created fantastically-decorated boxes filled with fried chicken and all the fixin's. Sheriff Joe bought Daisy's and old friend Charley bought Evelyn's. The four of them went to a corner of the room to enjoy their meal. The weekly newspaper reported that "a fine time was had by all."

A couple of weeks later Daisy called with some gossip to share. Evelyn was all ears, so the gals got together. They were bored. The remnants of winter were pushing them toward adventure. This happened every spring. Maybe this year would provide them something great. Daisy certainly sounded excited!

"I talked to Mrs. Avery yesterday. She was in town shopping for a new spring hat. In passing, she mentioned that there are two new guests at the Springs Spa recovering from a winter illness that kept them from working at the Carter Ranch where they had been hired. Mr. Carter was paying for their recovery time at the Springs. The doctor had prescribed rest for at least two months. Mrs. Avery is providing them with wonderful meals and they swim in the naturally hot mineral water every day. They are feeling better every day. Mrs. Avery says they are quite handsome and somewhat bored. I think they would benefit from some entertainment." She quieted down to give Evelyn a chance to think it over.

"Daisy, what are you suggesting?" asked Evelyn.

"I think they would enjoy some card games. Everyone likes to look through your stereopticon. Your collection of cards is extraordinary. Mrs. Avery says one of them is quite musical and plays some on their old piano. Do you ever consider duets when you play the violin?" Daisy thought she had suggested enough to keep Evelyn interested in her plan.

"What would be our excuse for driving to the Springs? We can't just drive up and say, 'Hello, I'm Daisy, I'm Evelyn.'"

With a twinkle in her eye, Daisy said, "Maybe we need to drive the Model T for a test. That would work for starters."

Evelyn tilted her head to the side, something she usually did when Daisy came up with an idea that didn't set quite right. When Daisy spotted the tilt, she reminded Evelyn, "Just how long has it been since you heard from Harry?"

"Oh, all right! I guess it can't hurt to take a drive up the river," said Evelyn as she pulled on her gloves and headed out the door. This was the day Evelyn and Daisy would meet Nigel and Alvin. Mrs. Avery introduced them and served everyone a glass of lemonade with her famous sugar cookies.

CHAPTER TWENTY-TWO

Clive took Saturday off. The middle of March looked promising. The cattle found some green grass to supplement the hay Clive pitched from the wagon every morning. The team knew where to go to distribute the feed, but some mornings Pa managed to go along and drive for Clive.

Evelyn called Daisy. "We seem to be taking a day off from work today. Would you like to venture up to the Springs again? I am looking for buttercups and other wildflowers to press and dry for note cards to use as gifts. Maybe Nigel and Alvin would like to join us on a wildflower hunt."

"Evelyn, you have the best ideas! Mother is watching the shop for me today so I am free as a bird." As usual, Daisy was up for adventure, especially if it included entertaining Alvin, who was recovering from his winter illness.

"I will pick you up at 9:30. Should we bring a picnic basket?" Evelyn asked.

"Good idea, but don't forget warm sweaters and blankets to sit on. After all, it is just a warm day in March, bound to be bookended by cold weather front and back," cautioned Daisy.

The two men seemed genuinely pleased when Daisy and Evelyn arrived. They entered into gathering the flowers and carefully saving them to press. After lunch they just wanted to lie on the warm blankets and visit, Alvin, the talker, and

Nigel, the tall rather quiet one with a head of dark curly hair. Evelyn looked Nigel over and decided "handsome" was a word that applied very nicely to him. She was curious about his background, age, education, and the family members left in England. But she rather forgot to ask all her questions when they were together and just enjoyed his presence.

Mrs. Avery offered them an early supper, so the ladies could drive home before dark.

"What a pleasant day," babbled Daisy as she squeezed in the shotgun seat and let Alvin close the door.

"Please come again. This spa gets very boring during the weeks of our recovery. You bring us a bright light. How about next Saturday?" Nigel asked.

"Maybe that will work. I'll call and leave a message with Mrs. Avery," promised Evelyn.

Alvin cranked the Model T and the ladies drove down the road.

CHAPTER TWENTY-THREE

Evelyn wondered if Pa sensed that her trips to the Springs were more than just a passion for wildflowers. Her collection of cards were quite lovely and she provided a display for the spring bazaar at church. The money raised was still designated for African orphans, but the threats of world poverty seemed foremost in the minds of the ranchers and miners of the John Day Valley. Evelyn realized the men who interested her were probably too old to be called into a war if the United States entered one. Then as she thought about it, both men had come from England and were probably not American citizens.

What was happening here? Was she comparing Harry to Nigel? Harry proposed by mail. Nigel had not proposed at all, but he looked at her with that special expression she found appealing. It was time for her to get her wits about her.

She reread part of a lovely letter Harry had written previously. She felt he may have not received one of her replies to him because his next letter came in May.

Received in May of 1913:

How is the garden? Have the sweet peas made their appearance yet? That is work I do thoroughly enjoy. In fact, at home I took care of all the flowers, etc. In the border around the house I planted geraniums, asters and stocks with a blue verbena border. At this time of the year and in the fall I would put in hyacinths, tulips, etc. with a crocus or snowdrop border. Trained up the side of the house were Gloria roses which almost hid the stonework. Then in front and in the centre of the drive is a large riser which I generally planted in chrysanthemums and dahlias, carnations, etc., in between tea roses and along the sides of the drive which was of gravel, were rhododendrons, lilacs and other flowering shrubs. So you can bet there was lots of work to keeping it right. I do not know how it is now, not having heard for so long. My oldest brother, who is the only one at the home place, is like all farmers. The garden is the least of his troubles. Possibly his wife sees to that part and keeps him from forgetting. I must sound like a gentleman farmer to you, Louise.

Box 102
Oatman, Arizona
12th May, 1913

My Dearest Louise,

I wrote you ages ago, but alas, no reply. I just couldn't stand the suspense any longer, hence this note. I hope it is not owing to sickness, which I can hardly think probable as you are always so healthy. My sincere wish is that it is not so, but that you are feeling fine. Do please drop a line to say hello—for I am wearying to hear from you as you are my very dearest lady friend. If I do not hear soon, don't be surprised if you see me come knocking at your door. Possibly there would be more knocking with me the victim. Are you going to take a vacation this summer? If so where, for I sure would like to see you again.

By the way, how did Charlie Collier come out on the U.S. Marshall position? I hope that he succeeded for he is surely deserving and a good fellow. I surmise that you are quite elated to see Bryan Sec. of State. You remember how you wished that he would make a good showing for the Presidency when Taft was elected. I see by the paper that the Japanese are trying to make it interesting with the U.W. regarding the alien law of Calif. It looks as tho the Japs are looking for an excuse for war.

There is not much startling news of the camp times. Everything is about normal. In fact, it is always the same. The last dance of the Social Club takes place on the 20th. How I wish you could be here to see how very enjoyable they really are. There are very few young ladies in camp, but the dances are always well attended by married couples. Also, quite a few come over from Goldroads. Then on the 30th the Oatman Band are going to give a dance. They expect to have their uniforms by that time, so, I guess they will be out in their war paint for sure. The band is quite a new thing, just having started about two months ago. I think that there are 25 pieces in it and are getting along fine. They have given two open air concerts which were very much enjoyed by the Oatmanites.

Oh yes! There is more in the exciting line which happened Friday night. A saloon was held up—also all the games—the hold-up got away with about $1500. The same night the Needles stage upset, breaking one fellow's leg. That is about all the startling news. The mine still

*runs along in the same old way, producing about the usual
amount of gold per month, around $100,000 — sometimes
more — seldom much less. Everything is lovely, barring the
weather, which is getting mighty tropical. Gee! How I long
for the tall pines, such as Strawberry Lake. I would like to
spend a week or so there this summer. Would you join me,
Louise? That would surely make it perfect. But! Possibly
you have a beau which would naturally mean that I would
not be wanted. I would sure like you to have one, but am
conceited enough to wish that it were I, as I think we are
just at the right age, don't you? If I remember your last
letter rightly you said that we were too set in our ways.
Don't you think you exaggerated and stretched it just a
little bit? I think you were joking, Evelyn.*

*Has George still got the meat market yet? If so, I hope
that he is doing well. By the way, where and how are the
Roberts family? I have not heard from them since they left
Portland Country. And your friend Daisy, is she getting
any better? I sincerely trust that she is. Tell her hello for
me, Louise. Now I must say good night with my very best
wishes etc., hoping that you are fine and dandy and that
you will write soon.*

*Yours very sincerely,
Harry*

*Is Harry again asking me to marry him? We beat around
the bush about our ages, interests, dispositions. Does he have
enough money saved? Do I care? Would he feel subservient to
come to me here on the ranch? Would I be able to forgive him
if he took me away to less comfortable circumstances? Mining
is in his blood. A family ranch surrounded by family members*

is a confining sort of place. Would he be happy held here, doing things the way my dad insists? After all, Harry is a 38-year-old man who has come from one continent to another, worked his way around the U.S. and found his niche, which has included cyanide poisoning. How is his health? What about my health? Am I too old for child-bearing?

Never-ending practical questions reared their ugly heads again.

In the meantime, she hired Nigel to work on the ranch when he finished his recovery at the Springs. Clive and Nigel kept the place operating nicely to Pa's expectations. Evelyn did write Harry, but it was July before she received a reply.

Evelyn understood about Nigel's health. Shortly after coming to work for Carter, he had been diagnosed with TB. He received medicine and the doctor's care for the first month and was then instructed to rest for six weeks before returning to work. This explained the prolonged visit at the Springs.

He seemed such a handsome gentleman to Evelyn as she drove up the river to see him every week. As his strength returned, they would take walks around the pools and in the woods. He would boost her over the stile that bridged the little stream of hot water. Evelyn was aware that his strength had returned and he would need to be back to work.

Roy Carter had filled the position he held for Nigel's return. He wanted a way out of paying the bond he held. Evelyn drove to Indian Creek to Carter's pace and made an offer that agreed to an arrangement to pay off the rest of the bond in exchange for his work at the Martin place. Plans were made for Nigel to move from the Springs to the Martin ranch.

The Imperial Hotel,
Portland, Oregon
July 16, 1913

My dearest Evelyn,

I was very pleased to get your very nice letter a few days ago, it having been forwarded on to L.A. It did seem good to see that old familiar handwriting as it is years since I heard from you. I have left Oatman, the hot climate was getting the best of me. It was 114 degrees in the shade, there being several cases of sun stroke. I would like to stay in Oregon for a while at least and try to get back to normal again. I expect to be in Portland several days. Then, I am going to do some work on some mining claims I have in So. Oregon. After that I really do not know where I will be, but, if I should leave Oregon again, I do wish that I could see you again, Evelyn (my eyes being hungry for the feast).

Who do you think I saw in L.A.? Jack Galbraith. I met him on the car so Monday night I called at his home and had a mighty fine visit. Mrs. J. is very nice indeed. I enjoyed talking over old times. Now I must shut up and get busy as I want to get out of Portland today. Tell Daisy hello.

With my very best love, yours as ever,
Harry

(Write soon Evelyn, please. Excuse haste. Enclosed are a few snapshots

Well, my letter has chased Harry around the country.

CHAPTER TWENTY-FOUR

The Comet Mine,
Galice, Oregon,
Sunday Eve 26th Oct. '13

My dearest Evelyn,

I have been going to write you for several days. I finally have gotten started. How very glad I was to get your welcome letter. It arrived in Portland after I had gone, but it eventually found me. I surely did feel good to get it as my thoughts often drift back to Prairie and of you. No doubt you will be somewhat surprised to learn that I'm still in Oregon. I am doing my annual assessment work upon the claims. About a month ago I bought my partner out. He was up here with me, but when he got the money and settled up, he left for Idaho. I've been alone ever since. I intend going ahead and doing as much work as I can to show the ledge at several places, so have some cross cutting to do. Gee! But it is lonesome up here. My nearest neighbors are about an hour's walk from me, over the mountains and again I do not like this cooking and dishwashing. It takes up so much of a fellow's time and

further more I would prefer a lady cook, as everything
tastes so much better. I know that yours would, Evelyn,
how I wish that you were here to give me a few pointers.
Better still; take the job off my hands. Ha Ha. I would be
happy and satisfied with life then. The claims are looking
pretty good and I hope to make a little something out of
them. As it was, with the partner, I saw no show so decided
to try it alone. I don't go much on these male partners
anyway. I would much rather prefer the other sex, but
seemingly at that I'm slow for getting her (seeing that I
want a particular one and her only).

I had a very nice trip north. I called at Los Angeles,
staying there about two weeks as I stood a possible show
of getting into the oil mining, but they were too slow in
getting started. Yes, I had a dandy visit with the Galbraiths.
He was very nice and Mrs. G. was exceptionally fine. I
enjoyed her immensely. Then I took the boat (Yale) from
L.A. to San Francisco, visiting in Berkeley a while, then
went down to central Calif. to Stockton , thence to Sutter
Creek, Angels Camp and Jackson on the mother lode, as
it is called. Curtis, a friend of mine with whom I have
worked on two different properties, wanted me to go into
the mine promoting business with him. He had taken leases
on two mines close to Angels Camp, however, it did not
look too feasible to me so I didn't take up his proposition.
After visiting with him a while and seeing the country in
his auto, I came back to Berkeley, then took the Beaver for
Portland. How I often wished that you could have been
visiting there also at the same time for I sure would have
enjoyed seeing you again.

So you were expecting yours truly knocking at your
door? I can assure you Louise, there is nothing that would

give me greater pleasure. The anticipation at seeing the young lady on the inside would have gratified a longing and pleasure that my feelings have craved forever since I was at Prairie. I saw you the day I left and you often bob up in my mind's eye. I hope that it may sometime be replaced by the original.

I surmise that Charley Collier, wife and family are in Portland ere this. Personally, I think he did a wise thing of course. I do not know the lady he married, but think that his own judgment will verify that she was the only one—at least I do hope so—as it is a treat to see a happy couple. I don't think that single life has the real charms of married life, as in nearly all cases, widowers and widows always remarry, which is proof in itself. No one is too old as in J.W. Mack's case. By the way, did you and Daisy take your vacation trip to Pendleton Round-up? Or did the school commencing put a stop to your plans? That certainly would have made a dandy outing for you. I feel sure that you two would have enjoyed it thoroughly.

When are they (she and Will) going to be wed, Louise? Or do you know? I'm mighty pleased to hear that her health is so much improved. I remember you said some time ago that she was so very much run down. Tell her hello for me, please. Now, I think that I've given you all the news for once so will say goodnight hoping that I'll be favored with a letter from you very soon, Louise. I enjoy them immensely. In fact, above all else, next to the original, or writer. Also that you are feeling fine and dandy and happy.

From yours very sincerely,
Harry

8 Nov. '13

Dearest Evelyn,

I have just received very sad news, since writing you—
the death of my youngest brother Herbert—he died after an
operation for appendicitis. He took sick on the Friday and
called the Dr. who visited him that day, twice on Saturday and
Sunday. On Monday he ordered an operation, but he was too
late so mortification had already set in. He died the following
Thursday. It sure is sad news to me. I thought so much of him.
He had just been married but a short while and was settling
nicely in business, having a large meat market in the south
of England. Apparently there was no hope from the time of
the operation. He has always enjoyed the best of health, being
strong and husky. It is hard to realize that he has truly gone.
Please excuse, more tonight, and that you will write soon.

Prairie City, Oregon
November 26, '13

My dear Harry,

How very sorry I was to hear of your brother's passing.
Your trip home was certainly marred with sadness. Your letter
did give me a picture of what your life in England had been. I
could see how much love you had for your siblings. I am sure
they would have liked to keep you there with them, but I know
you are a dedicated miner in this "new world" as they say.

Pa and I are keeping you and your family in our prayers
during your time of mourning.

Fondly,
Evelyn

CHAPTER TWENTY-FIVE

In November, Evelyn wrote a more cheerful letter to Harry with all the news and complimenting the pictures he had sent.

Galice. Oregon,
Dec 18th, '13

My dear Evelyn,

Your letter came a few days ago and was greatly enjoyed. I am sorry you were interrupted while writing. I should have liked to have heard all you had to say as you apparently were happy and in a very jolly mood, surmising from your remarks regarding your cooking, etc. Before I can fully decide with you in that respect, I'm from Missouri, Evelyn as the saying goes and will have to be shown. I feel sure that I would enjoy it immensely and would be most willing to take the chance of surviving a lifetime, let alone two weeks. Ha ha.

I am glad that you liked the pictures and may say I feel very highly elated at your comments upon same, as to the youthful appearance. Personally, I had not discovered it. Weren't you a trifle flattering, Louise? However, I cannot lose the opportunity of thinking that you were sincere.

So, thank you ever so much indeed. In replying to your enquiry regarding the fountain of youth, I may say that all I can attribute it to is my devotion to a certain young lady to whom I am just now writing. You see that you can help me out to the fullness of my desire, as you wished to speak a good word for me, your assistance in all I require. So, Louise, just speak a good word to Evelyn, she being the one and only.

I am so very sorry to hear of Daisy's sad loss, that of the death of her mother. It must surely be dreadfully hard for Daisy to bear. Really, I believe your suggestion regarding her would help her materially to forget her troubles. She has my deepest sympathy.

It is snowing to beat the band today. About 4 inches fell last night. There is no telling when it will quit once it gets started, but up until yesterday, Dec. month has been fine, just like summer. I may go to Portland next week to see my old or would-be partner and try and get this business straightened out. It will just be for 2 or 3 days. Then I will be back here for 2 months.

I hope that you will excuse this short note as I want to wish you many happy returns of your birthday. Also, the Yuletide greetings with an overflowing around of jollity and good things and that in 1914 you will have all your heart desires. Good night Evelyn, hoping you are fine and dandy and that I'll hear from you soon.

Yours most sincerely,
Harry

P.S. Be careful under the mistletoe. Ha Ha.

Evelyn's next reply was a brief letter—she was afraid to say yes. After all, this had been a correspondence courtship. Harry needed to come there in person if his proposals were serious. Then there was Nigel, the handsome ranch hand who was strong and knew how to do ranch work. His presence that caused a rattling of her insides when he came to the house. It was like the old saying, "One bird in the bushel is worth two in the bush." Evelyn had a strong feeling Nigel was willing to propose marriage.

CHAPTER TWENTY-SIX

Stewart, B.C.
15th Aug. 1914

My dear Evelyn,

I was mighty glad to get your letter when I came down to Eleven Mile Road House. I am going to write you a note before I go back to the Yellowstone. I have just gotten through assaying and it is now after 10:00 P.M. I must hit the trail by 7:00 A.M. tomorrow as it is an all day hike until noon. I follow a blazed trail. After that it is above timber line and the travelling is upon snow with glaciers practically in every direction. I go along one that is about ½ mile wide, the length I would hate to have to determine. It is a very beautiful sight from the Yellowstone Property — looking over the glacier near at hand and numerous lakes in the distance, some with immense floating icebergs showing their delicate blue in the sun. It has been delightfully cool. Sorry you couldn't have shared some of it, Evelyn, for I note that you have had oppressive heat in Prairie. I surmise that this month will end my trips to that property as the snow, I believe, begins to fall next month. I have 5 men working up there, principally surface work, and 2 men working on another property near Eleven Mile. I take the samples and assay them and keep the company posted. I have a cabin which is situated right on the side of the line, separating B.C. from Alaska, where I have my assay outfit. I make the trip about every two weeks. I do not expect that this work will last very much longer as I have most of my part completed.

I am very sorry to hear of the accident which happened to your father and aunt in your Model T, tho it is sure good news to learn that both are progressing nicely. How could they do otherwise with such a sweet, good nurse? Don't you know I had almost come to the conclusion that you were still celebrating as you said you'd write soon as the celebration was over. You did not mention the Fourth of July. I hope that you had an enjoyable time.

I have just heard that the boat has been taken off and practically everything tied up owing to the war. The merchants here are getting their goods by gasoline launch from Ketchikan so I guess I'm doomed to stay in this neck of the woods until the trouble is over. I have not had a newspaper since July so I really do not know the true state of affairs tho! They must be serious from the existing conditions right now.

By the way, how is your dear friend Mrs. Avery? I hope she is fine and dandy and still married. Is Will Nicklaus still holding the fort at the Dixie? I would like to see him make a killing there.

Now, Evelyn, I must shut up and go to bed. Hoping you are feeling at your best again. I was sure sorry to hear of you having had hay fever. It is, I surmise, a miserable thing. Kindly excuse this hurried note. I am anxiously looking forward to your newsy letter. So long for the present.

Evelyn sent Thanksgiving greetings in the form of an extended letter to Harry, a letter sent when times were stressed, war threatened, and most folks had a get-on-with-life mentality. Mail was slow; letters were like ships that pass in the night.

Letter received from Galice, Oregon, Jan. 6, 1915

My dear Evelyn,

You are a precious darling, the dearest sweetest and adorable girl I know, Ha Ha. I enjoyed the long card immensely, the best ever. How fortunate and tickled I am that I had already written you hoping that you have received my letter long before this, Evelyn. Hope you had a dandy good time Xmas. We are having genuine Yuletide weather, snow galore.

Many thanks for your kind wishes. I am writing this note in the P.O. so kindly excuse more at present. I so enjoyed your chiding that I couldn't refrain from writing a line of appreciation.

So long with my very sincere and best wishes. Hoping you are fine and dandy and that I'll hear from you soon.

Yours as ever,
Harry

P.S. It is sure worth a box of candy.

CHAPTER TWENTY-SEVEN

With Nigel ensconced in the old log cabin for the winter another year of work began on the ranch. Clive still came to work half days during the winter as Nigel needed help to feed the cattle. Evelyn found herself cooking breakfasts for Nigel and Pa and noon meals for all three men. At night it was just Pa and Nigel again. Evelyn sighed with fatigue in the evenings, too tired to sit by the lamp to read or sew. Nigel spent time visiting with Pa. He seemed determined to learn all the information available about the ranch. He was strong, but obviously had not learned how to work with the land. Some of his statements sounded like his education had come from time on the docks in England, loading the goods that country shipped around the world.

Talk of the War filled the conversations taking place at Marsh's old store. Habit drew the old timers of the area there to shop. The meat market that had been so proudly built with a bull's head carved of stone above the door was transformed to an auto repair shop. Patrons drove up to the front, inside the building, and straight on out the back to the side street when their cars were repaired.

Other changes to the little city included a new high school built across the river. Two good bridges connected both banks. The Methodist church sat proudly on its site with a park in front and Strawberry Mountain in the background. The train depot was overseer to the turn-around that sent the single gauge transporter back to Baker City twice a week.

Evelyn tried to write all this in a letter to Harry, but she wondered if he would really be interested. She found his move to Canada puzzling. For a man who had professed his love of Eastern Oregon and a desire to become a rancher since she met him in 1909, the move out of the country seemed strange. Was he concerned about his home country and the results of the war? Everyone was sure both countries would soon be at war.

Evelyn sensed the feelings of the Prairie Cityites when she was in town last week. There was a sense of anger and fear. Someone was prepared to string up a figure that looked like a German officer. They pretended he was the Kaiser, to be burned in effigy. Evelyn thought the whole thing was actually pointless, but it certainly showed how angry the people in Eastern Oregon were. Westerners don't like to have their freedoms, or anyone else's, jeopardized. Evelyn knew her nephew, George's oldest boy, was considering joining the army as soon as it was available to him. The German code of war conduct hit the news and rattled the ordinary folks around the Valley, as well as around the nation. Evelyn finally decided to discuss the issues with Harry. The war in Europe seemed to be spilling over its boundaries. Evelyn had seen a newsreel when she attended a movie on her last trip to Portland. She found it very disturbing to see the war moving in front of her in a movie. She thought if Harry had been writing regularly, she would discuss the European situation with him. His reasonable explanations gave her comfort. She decided to write a serious letter to Harry without the gossip that normally filled her pages.

Prairie City, Oregon
May 10, '15

Dear Harry,

I wish you were here to discuss the war and other serious matters. I find it all so troubling. The Prairie Cityites are anti-German. It is so bad that the few German families in the Valley are no longer welcome at many of the homes in town. Even at church they sit in a section on the right side near the back. Of course, these good people are not responsible for the atrocities of the German army, but prejudice is a terrible thing.

The sinking of the Lusitania proves that Germany will sink any ship they consider their enemy. The whole affair was terrifying. The only thing worse was the use of poison gas at Ypres. The Oregonian had a sickening picture of allied soldiers blinded by gas. How inhumane!

I fear that the United States will join the allies in this battle. Our good men will go to war across the ocean so far from home. The paper said the troops at Ypres were choking and so frightened they ran from the front line. The Canadians were the only ones to tough it out to the end. I am glad you are safely in the hills of British Columbia mining and not on a front line somewhere.

The rest of life here goes on as usual. Your beloved sweet peas are up and preparing to put on a grand show in our garden.

Sincerely,
Evelyn

567 Hornsby Street
Vancouver, B.C.

My Dear Evelyn,

You may write me at the above address c/o Canadian Mining Exploration Co. My replies will be sparse as my current work keeps me confined and very busy. Speaking of my current work, I hesitate to say much about it. Anything war related is very hush hush and I have been recruited to share my expertise about surviving the results of being gassed. As you know, my work with Cyanide involved some danger and I do have a good deal of information on the subject. My alliance is still with England and now Canada. The results of gassing can be somewhat contained with immediate use of oxygen. I am not free to discuss the project I am involved in. It may even mean I will have to go to England or France to implement what we have been experimenting with. Please know that a visit with you in Prairie would be my desire, but men of honor must do their work when it is needed.

With every good wish I remain yours,
Harry

This was the last letter Evelyn saved. A Christmas card addressed to Mr. Harry Smithworth, 567 Hornby St., Vancouver, B.C., c/o Canadian Mining Exploration Co., was also saved but never mailed. Evelyn's father died quietly at home, April 2, 1916.

EVELYN'S STORY 1916

After Pa died, I brought out all the bookwork for the ranch. My brothers and sister met in the kitchen around the old table Pa had made for the family way back when he and Ma were married. It had served us well for many years. When I was born in 1880 it was full of children. I was number nine and some of them were on the verge of leaving home. Grandmother Mary Martin died the same year I was born. Maybe I ended up taking her place at the table. Everyone missed our Pa and hated to see him go, but it was the worst for me because I had lived here taking care of Pa's needs since 1900. He was not an old-fashioned man, but he was tight with his money, so I was required to keep a good set of books about our affairs.

Everyone expected their share of things and money, especially the money. Pa had arranged to help his children as they grew and left home. He always looked for bargains in land and livestock. His one adventure into the hotel business had been nice for me in my younger years, but it no longer interests me now. My ledger books were tidy and accurate. The court had no trouble deciding the probate to divide the assets.

Pa had made it clear to everyone a number of years ago that I was to inherit the homeplace and arrange to run it, so after the house, land, equipment and animals were taken out, each of us inherited our share of the money saved in the bank. I wrote checks to each brother and my sister for $3,975.42. I kept my inherited amount in my personal bank account. We held a separate ranch account with some funds for operating expenses. I have a crew of two who receive wages every month. My brothers all have families with children old enough to do the work on their places. Everyone went home happy with their checks, giving me hugs as they left.

The house quieted then. The ticking of Ma's clock could be heard through the silence. I remembered to wind it for tomorrow's chime. When Pa passed, we laid him on the closed-in back porch because it was cooler to keep his body until the family all arrived. The young children were wide-eyed to see their grandpa lying there so still. I tried to avoid the porch for the days he was there as I found it no comfort to have his body there.

After the funeral and the divvying up of the property, life began to be more normal, but I felt tired in every bone of my body.

April 10, 1916

Ma's clock struck the hours throughout the night and reminded me when it was six o'clock. My habit of forty years could not be broken. Sunlight streamed in the kitchen window as I cooked the oatmeal just as I always had. I made enough for Nigel when he came in from the morning chores. He ate up without asking me a lot of questions, although I knew he was curious about my plans. I made a secret vow to share some thoughts with him before the end of the week.

April 15, 1916

Those of us who get our living from the land are spared little time to mourn a death or celebrate a birth. The land calls and demands our attention. I had Nigel come to plant the vegetable garden. I remember how Pa used to lay out straight rows by riding his hoe like a stick horse up and down the patch. Then we would plant the peas, lettuce, beets, and carrot seeds, pull some soil over ant tap it down. We would spade up holes for potatoes and I would drop the four seed potatoes in each hole as Pa held the shovel. This time I had to explain to Nigel exactly how to do it. I suspect when he lived in England, he never planted a vegetable garden. Maybe he didn't own any land. When I ask him questions about his life before he came to Prairie City, he smoothly changes the subject and I get no answers.

I guess Nigel's previous life is no real business of mine. He is a willing worker and learns our ways of ranching quickly. I find myself depending on him just as if he were a part of the family. Sometimes when it gets hot, I see him pull off his outer shirt and tie it around his waist. If he is not wearing his long johns, I see a bare chest and sinewy muscles. None of the Martin men ever took off their shirts for field work so I find myself staring from the porch. Of course, he always puts his shirt on before he comes to the house for meals.

April 21, 1916

Yesterday I asked Nigel over to the house to help me move some things. It was time to box Pa's clothes and personal possessions and air out his room. He and my mother had slept in the downstairs bedroom for many years and Pa stayed in the same room the rest of his life. Now that I am the ranch owner, I am experiencing a bit of spoiled power and think I will move my room downstairs. It won't be hard to give up the climb of the narrow stairs with the twist halfway where the steps are narrow, almost dangerous. I put Nigel's muscles to good use toting furniture to new locations and humping boxes to the attic. After I sort through my girlish possessions, I'll have him back over to move my things downstairs.

April 22, 1916

Today's work in my room brought back over thirty years of memories. The worst, which I could not forget, was when my brother Eddie rode off after the fight with that school teacher. I understood what shame and sadness do to a family, but for me, I had lost my playmate turned brother-protector-and-confidant. No one talked to me about it. I just listened to the adult conversation and drew my young girl conclusions about it, about being deserted by my brother who was so afraid for himself.

Then I folded up the letters from Harry that were still in my room. His last note about the war effort he was involved in while in Canada made him seem like a hero. But that was the last I heard of him. After such a long correspondence, I think he may have returned to England and died in the war. I would be devastated to think he had found another woman and married. I would only have myself to thank for that! I will put the red box in with the old ranch records (Pa never threw a scrap of paper away) and seal them shut. I will never have time to sort those records. No one else will want them, but I will know where those letters from Harry are in case I ever feel compelled to find them. After two full years, I have pushed him to the back of my mind as an "interlude of my unmarried era."

Why did I write it that way? What a funny thing for me to say. Is a desire for marriage on my mind again? As soon as I seal and tie these boxes I'll get Nigel up here to do the heavy work.

May 16, 1916

Decision time! I called Fred Tillman today and arranged for indoor plumbing. He will be out here to the ranch tomorrow to look at the house and the land near it. We need to decide where to place the toilet, sink and bathtub in the house and where to dig for the septic tank. There is lots of work involved to put a bathroom in an old house that never had one. But one trip to the Imperial Hotel was enough to convince me we needed one at home. Pa just never wanted to spend the money. I have a little undesignated money, and I plan to designate it to this plumbing project. I may even decide to add electricity at the same time.

May 17, 1916

Tonight I plan to dream about the bathroom. In the morning I should have it all drawn out in my head. We have a place to wash up on our back porch. When men sleep in the bunkhouse they can still use the outhouse. Fred suggested putting the bathroom on the far end of the porch. That would require building in a room with insulation and I would have to go across the house to get to it. My idea is to take some space from the downstairs bedroom and build a little hall between it and the fireplace. I know Nigel is willing to work on this project, but my brother George is a wonderful carpenter and I would ask him to help with it. He and Alice have just put a bathroom in their house and it worked out just fine. We are both going to bring electricity to our places and the schoolhouse up the lane. What an improvement that will be. Writing in my journal will be more pleasant with good light in the evenings. I am getting so excited, I probably won't sleep at all tonight.

June 3, 1916

I think I will write a bathroom update. George agreed to help out with the project. He knew how to make the little hall match the rest of the house. It looks as if it has always been there. He was able to avoid some of the standard pitfalls of adding a bathroom to an old farm house. George is a bit stubborn about how things should be done. Nigel wanted to be the big doer on the whole project. I could hear words and growling between them. Nigel did not like being designated as the helper. I tried to stay out of the fray.

A big hole for the septic tank needed to be dug so George sent Nigel to do that job. The only good thing about that was that Nigel ripped off his shirt when he got hot and I was treated to his lovely physique. Oops. I am reminding myself right here to keep this journal stored away in case someone should choose to read my private thoughts.

Tomorrow I will invite Daisy up to see our ne bathroom.

June 6, 1916

Daisy finally came to the ranch. We had not had a private visit for a long time. Now that she is married to the sheriff, she is full of gossip about the goings on in Prairie City. She even asked how I liked having that handsome Nigel living here. I poo-pooed her and said he was just a hired hand, but we have been friends so long it was hard to fool her. I told her she was only here to pass judgment on the bathroom, which met with her approval. Then she wondered if Nigel would be allowed in to use it. A good point was made that cleaning up in a regular bathtub would surpass the dragging of the big washtub out and filling it with water from the kitchen.

I daresay, Daisy left me with some things to think about. I also knew George would disapprove of having Nigel in the house. The bathroom incident brokered ugly feelings between them. This may be one of those nights when I get a limited amount of sleep.

June 30, 1916

Well, I did it. I invited Nigel to move into one of the upstairs bedrooms. In a couple of weeks we will be filling the log bunkhouse with a haying crew. Nigel, as a full-time hand, would be the supervisor, so to speak, so it was a logical move. I have some mixed feelings: someone else occupying the house will feel good, many nights have felt lonely since Pa passed. On the other hand, having Nigel right above my bedroom may be disconcerting. The room is large. My brothers used it like a dormitory when everyone was home. I could add another crew member during haying as Nigel's roommate. That is a good plan to make the move less awkward.

I spend too much time worrying about "what people think" and "how things look."

                                        July 4, 1916

Independence Day! The worries of the war in Europe put a damper on the usual celebration. The church yard was used as a picnic potluck location. As in years past, we Martins fried chicken, made potato salads and chocolate cakes to take to town. We waited around for Bill Hopper to show off his fireworks. Now that nearly everyone has cars to drive, we can make a trip home in the dark pretty easy.

Nigel and I drove to town for the festivities. I ran into Daisy who pulled me aside and asked if I ever thought about Harry anymore. I think I gasped because I had not thought about Harry in a long time. I told her, "No."

I didn't tell her I found myself thinking about Nigel instead.

                                      August 14, 1916

What a busy month. Haying took a long time as we had an inexperienced crew and Nigel in charge. He had never really been a boss, although he wanted to be. He believed he could get men and boys who had not operated haying equipment to do the job. The money he saved us with low wages was eaten up in the work that had to be repeated. George even brought over some of his extra fence panels to fence the haystacks. Nigel was offended, but I was grateful.

At last we are finished; my hay fever is abated. Nigel's roommate has moved on to another job, with more knowledge of ranching than he came with.

September 9, 1916

Nigel and I have spent a month in the house. I fix the food and he handles the outdoor chores. In the evenings I enjoy reading or doing handwork under my new electric floor lamp. Nigel is a jigsaw puzzle fan so we have one going on the library table most of the time. He gets mail occasionally, but never shares any information or leaves the letters lying around. I admit, I would be curious to read one of them, but of course I won't, not even if he leaves one out. I appreciate my privacy and he deserves his also.

The other day he said he hated to climb the stairs to his room. I didn't know if he was just tired, or if he was trying to suggest something more. Nigel is five years younger that I, so he should not be tired. He looks the picture of vim and vigor with his broad shoulders and his curly dark hair. Since moving into the house he has kept a clean shaven face, which I appreciate.

Pa's long beard had never appealed to me. It was old fashioned, a bit smelly, and often harbored bits of food from a previous meal. It was a part of his persona and I never suggested he shave it off. Beards are not in vogue now and I certainly am glad!

October 1, 1916

Our apples are picked. The jam is made. I think I made far too much to feed Nigel and myself. I will use the extra for Christmas presents, not for the children, just for the grown-ups. I like to look forward to the holiday season. The church bazaar and the sharing of gifts add to the warm feeling of the season. This year I am afraid President Wilson will ask the nation to join the war to help our European allies. It seems we have been in one skirmish or another since the turn of the century. If we enter this war, our young men will be sent to fight. I know so many boys in the Valley as our ancestors settled here as pioneers.

Nigel would be a different matter as he is not an American citizen and certainly out of reach for England. This thought just ran through my mind. This journal holds many thoughts that just run through my mind.

December 25, 1916

I have been invited to spend Christmas Day with George and Alice. It is our custom to prepare a very special meal and watch the children enjoy their gifts. Nigel was not invited. I don't know his feelings about Christmas. He never accepts my invitation to accompany me to church, even on potluck days. I'm sure George is bitter about the way Nigel operates the ranch as if it belonged to him instead of to me. I admit, he is rough on the machinery. Next spring I expect they will have words over how the irrigation is done. We have always had a schedule between the ranches about opening and closing the head gates.

I plan to bring the disagreements to an end. I know the Martin family will not be happy to hear it, but I plan to marry Nigel when he asks. He has made various suggestions and I know a proposal is forthcoming. When Nigel is my husband, he will be the owner and operator of the ranch. There will be an end to the disagreements because the family will not fight with my husband as they all want my happiness.

January 2, 1917

I was right. Nigel asked me to marry him last night. The start of a new year and a new life for us. We have kept house for the last six months so I have a good idea what my life will be like. Five years of letter writing left me an "old maid." I am ready to pass the part of maiden lady by and claim a handsome dark-haired man as mine. I asked Nigel if a trip to the county court house would be an adequate ceremony. I think he was relieved not to include my family and a preacher. A wedding trip is out of the question because in January we have to be home to feed hay to the cattle.

January 6, 1917

I called the court house and made arrangements for a marriage ceremony with Judge Rankin. His calendar held a spot for us on January 10. I have to admit I am a little fluttery in the stomach with the excitement of it all. I have waited a very long time.

My next call was to Daisy to see if they would stand up with us. I'm not sure Nigel wanted the sheriff to join us, but

I thought having him a witness would be a good omen. I also think January 10 is a good date, easy to remember so Nigel will never forget our anniversary. I wonder if he has a ring for me. A nice little gold band would be nice if he has enough money to buy one. I think I will go see Daisy for a new hat to perk up my Sunday dress and winter coat.

Even better than all this, a sweet baby of our own would make my life complete, another Eddie to add to the family.

January 11, 1916

Nigel moved into the downstairs bedroom and joined me for our first night together. I hated that we had to get up to feed those cows early today, but a rancher's life looks to the land and livestock first. I fixed ham and eggs for breakfast to make the morning special.

Dreading to make my first phone call, I heaved a big sigh and headed for the phone. When Alice answered, I asked to speak to George. My statement that Nigel and I were married was met with silence. Brother George had no words to express himself. I'm sure he had plenty to share with Alice after he hung up on me. I would just give him time to get used to the idea. Calling Nigel his brother-in-law will probably never happen.

February 18, 1916

This has been a cold winter. The snow settled in the fields and turned to ice, crunching under the wagon tires as we drove to feed out the hay. Every day we chopped holes in the ice so the stock could drink. Even though we now have an electric refrigerator, we still filled the icehouse with blocks of ice packed in sawdust. This is another good year for ice skating on the ponds in the fields. I remember having such a good time with Harry when we did it years ago. Now, I have a husband who never puts on skates and I am staying off them this year as I am pregnant and plan to take good care of myself. The doctor says I am healthy and should have no trouble delivering a healthy baby. Then he goes on to remind me that I am nearly thirty-seven and have never had a child, a good reason to take very good care of myself. I have waited a long time to be a mother, so I will take no chances.

I am hoping for a boy because I know that would please Nigel and then I can name a boy after my favorite missing brother, Eddie.

Nigel used to look at me with a twinkle in his dark eyes. He liked that I was a tiny person. Being with me made him look big and strong, a man not to be messed with. Now my figure is beginning to change and I find him gazing out the window, not so often at me. I know his attention will change back to me in August, after our baby is born.

May 11, 1917

Spring came with a bang. Buttercups graced the hillsides like a saffron carpet. The lush green of the new grass belied the fate promised by the hard winter. It looks as if we will get the cows and calves to the mountain range early. The hay will grow and by the time harvest is over, we will welcome our new family member. I plan to have the baby in the hospital. Many children are still born at home, but the doctor recommends I come to town. It is fine with me because there is no one here to care for us except Nigel, and I have no idea how he would be with a baby. His hands match the rest of him, large and rough, ready to work.

I must record what happened last week. My brother Lee and our Pastor rode up Dixie to turn out a small herd of cows for pasture. Lee and Missy are good friends of the Pastor and his family, so they decided to make an outing of it. The wives packed a picnic, loaded the children into their car and drove to a meeting point up the mountain. It is a lovely spot where one can see the whole valley from the north side and have a grand view of Strawberry Mountain on the south. The mountains look blue from this spot. No wonder they are called the Blue Mountains. When one gets closer, they are just covered with many evergreens. When I was a little girl I used to wonder about it. Anyway, while the families picnicked, the horses got away. Sure that they had wandered a short distance, the men sent the ladies home in the car.

It was not a short distance. In fact, the men walked all the way home with no horses at all. So much for the theory that a horse will always find its way home. To add insult to injury, a reporter for the Blue Mountain Eagle heard the story and printed in for all to see. I think the preacher had to explain it to all on Sunday morning.

                                        June 25, 1917

I had to enter something humorous in my last journal entry so it will not be filled with gloom and doom. President Wilson has us entered in the war, saying we need to help Europe keep democracy. Everyone is sure he will institute a draft to fill an army with our men. Secretly I am very happy Nigel will not be eligible to go somewhere and fight. I need him here at home. George's oldest boy is joining up, off to basic training any day now.

I am aware that we are keepers of the land and the people in this Valley who share and care for one another. Sometimes I feel frustrated with the gossip that floats around us, but other times it seems like a cloak that protects us from the outside. If one boy from a ranch must leave for war, a neighbor or two will step in and fill the vacancy. I wonder if the citizens of war-torn Europe help each other the same way.

I feel "as big as a horse" to repeat the expression so often used around here. I no longer look petite. If no one sees me until the end of August, it will be soon enough. Alice's daughter will come help me during haying. I can already tell my feet are beginning to swell.

I wish Nigel showed more interest in our baby. I feel as if I am "going it alone."

September 2, 1917

I have just come home with our new baby. He is adorable, even when crying. I was glad to leave the hospital. The nurses could hear Nigel and me discussing names. We are not in agreement so our little boy is still unnamed. Nigel won't budge. He hates the name of Eddie for his son. "He will always be a little boy with that name. People will remember that his scared uncle ran away. Sidney John Hanson, now that's a proper name," he told me.

I gave in. Arguing with Nigel tears me apart, so I will just carry Eddie as a secret name in my heart.

October 14, 1917

We just heard the Americans have reached the Western Front. Maybe they can push the Germans back. Paris is in great danger. We continue with our chores of ranching and caring for the folks left here. The cloud of war colors all we do. I care for Sidney and take joy in his development. We are blessed to have our lovely son. Nigel looks at him, but is not much to pick him up or cuddle him as I do. "I'll wait till he gets bigger," he tells me. "Then he will be some help around this place."

November 20, 1917

I have just come home from the church where we are preparing gift bags for our soldiers. Everything must be sent by the end of the week in order to reach the trenches before Christmas. I want every soldier to have a package and a letter to open in case they have no family at home to send them a gift. Sidney goes with me and the members of the Ladies' Aid take turns holding him if he fusses. Daisy comes to help. I think she is a little jealous of my baby, that he was born first. She is pregnant now, so we will have children who are good friends, if she has a boy.

December 19, 1917

I am making a little bear for Sidney's first Christmas. It is very soft and a toy he may take to his bed, no button eyes. Nigel says boys don't need dolls, but I am holding my ground on this toy. Although boys need to grow up strong, they also need to be gentle and caring. I think Nigel will make him a man before his time. I hope we will come to an agreement on how to raise the boy. I know he will be frustrated if his mother and father do not agree. I also know Nigel will be the winner in any battle. He never talks about his childhood, but I think he grew up in the slums of London. He doesn't seem to be aware of our Santa Claus tradition.

One thing we agree on at holiday time is the food. A plum pudding always brings a smile to his face and reminds me of when we first met at the Springs. I was so shy and he so quiet and handsome. To capture the past may be more than a good morning's work for us.

We didn't butcher a hog this year, but George brought us one of his hams from his smokehouse. It promises to make us a wonderful Christmas dinner. Besides the three of us, we will have Nigel's cousin who has just arrived in the Valley. I think Nigel knew he was coming, but he didn't share the information with me. I am suspicious that Michael Hanson wrote ahead to see if he would be accepted here.

I find Michael to be very charming and agreeable. His manners are very nice and he is helpful. I would like it if he stayed with us as he would be a wonderful influence on Sidney as he matures. Maybe I am getting the cart before the horse, as people say. (Maybe he reminds me a bit of Harry, a well-mannered Englishman.)

January 23, 1918

Our boys are still in the trenches, and here at home we continue to pitch hay to the cows, feed the chickens, and do our other chores. I guess it is our way to keep the home fires burning. George is forty-six years old and he received a Selective Service card last year. Wilton Jones returned from his duty with a case of the shakes from being gassed near the German border. I would think the Germans would be worn out from fighting. It has been so long I can't even remember why we are fighting.

The Ladies' Aid project this year is to knit wool socks and scarves for the troops. I finish a set every week by knitting every night. The addition of electricity to our area has increased our productivity.

We have sold milk to a neighbor who has no cow. This source of income will probably come to a close as we have a new regulation that all milk cows must be tested. I'm sure our cows are fine, but Nigel has no intention to let the government tell him what to do with his cows. I guess the neighbors will have to go elsewhere.

March 31, 1918

Warm, windy days are perfect for kite flying. I took Sidney over to watch George's children fly the ones they had made. He clapped his little hands and giggled as they took off to the clouds. They were made from newspapers and scraps from George's carpentry shed. Sidney stands up by holding my hands and picking each foot up in the air. The bigger kids play with him when Alice gives me a cup of tea.

Tomorrow I will go to town to wish Daisy an April Fool's Day greeting. I wonder if she will remember that it was four years ago when the women of Oregon finally became legal voters. We high-tailed it to Canyon City to the county seat as soon as we heard. I wish my mother had been alive to see that day. She had become an advocate for Women's Rights. In fact, Eddie had used some of her information for the paper he wrote to finish high school, when he had the fight with the school teacher.

It would be so wonderful to find him.

August 8, 1918

George and Nigel continue to fight over the water. Both want to get it on the hay fields to get the feed growing again. In a couple of months we will be riding to bring the cattle home from the summer range. As usual our herds will have mixed and George will complain that our bulls are not as good as his and that next year's crop of calves will be poor quality. As I see it, this is not a provable point.

At the end of the month, Sidney will be a year old. I hope he will be taking steps alone by then. I am tired of answering that question, "Is Sydney walking yet?" I think I will keep him home here on the ranch until he can march down the main street of Prairie City by himself with his little chest pushed out and his head held high.

November 12, 1918

Sidney is walking! Even more important, the Germans have surrendered. Our boys from the Valley will be coming home. I am too excited to write in my journal tonight.

December 27, 1918

Nigel is watching Sidney make his way across the living room. Finally, he appreciates what his little boy can do. They spend time building with a set of blocks George and Alice gave Sidney for Christmas. They build a tower and then knock it down. They think that is great fun. It makes me remember that Eddie could never build with blocks to suit my father. It seemed to add to his frustration. Nigel is playing. I think he was right when he told me to let the little guy grow up so they could have some fun. I have learned I don't always have to have my own way.

   This journal is nearly full. I think I will store it away with my old autograph books. The nasty war is over. Time for new beginnings.

Evelyn Martin Hanson

1919

"Mama," called Sidney from the back seat of the new car.

"You walk, you talk, you are Mama's and Daddy's big boy," answered Evelyn as she drove home from town. She had just heard news that made her fly over the muddy gravel highway, wondering as she always did if the State of Oregon would ever get it paved. It would be a good post-war project to fix the roads since nearly everyone owned a car now.

Evelyn's stomach churned with excitement as she recalled the Ladies Aid meeting she had just attended. Bertha Collins had called her aside after telling everyone about the motor trip she had taken with Mr. Collins. Their stops in Montana to see relatives, miles of dry land through the Dakotas, finally reaching the big lakes of Minnesota. Bertha's mother lived in Minnesota and it had been "just grand" to see her again. When Bertha told a story, every aspect of it was "just grand." Finally, Bertha stepped to the side of the room and beckoned to Evelyn.

"Evelyn, I have been wanting to see you since we got home. It has been so busy at our place, I just couldn't get out to come calling. And then I thought Nigel would not be as interested in this information as you would. Mind you, we haven't spoken to anyone else about it," Bertha rattled on.

Eventually she did get to the point. "We decided to take a more southern route home, stopping in Iowa and Nebraska to look at farmland that was no better than what we have here. In one little town where we stopped for a noon meal, we saw a cook behind a partition who also came out to be our waiter. He had a most familiar look, but Mr. Collins and I could not place him. You know how it is when you forget someone's name and then it comes to you hours later? Well, we told him he looked familiar.

"He said we would never know if we had once been acquainted, that it wouldn't be worth our time to worry about it.

"With that he went back to the kitchen to fry up something for his next customer."

Bertha bounced Sidney on her knee as she continued her story. "It was the next day and we were miles down the road when Mr. Collins said, 'Ed Martin! It's been years, but that cook looked like Ed Martin!' Of course, it has been years, but I thought you might be interested in the resemblance we noticed."

"Do you remember the name of the restaurant?' Evelyn had asked.

"Dearie, no. I can't even remember the little town—maybe if I looked at a road map," Bertha said.

Sidney was getting restless and Evelyn thought Bertha's story would never end as she thought of more details of her trip. She thanked the woman, said her good-byes, and headed to the car with her son in tow. Maybe there was nothing to the gossip, but maybe it meant Eddie was alive somewhere, having a normal life.

In 1895 the Martin family had their lives turned topsy-turvy when Eddie left. They thought he would come back in a day or two, but there was no sign of him. A couple of weeks after, the Averys came down Strawberry Creek from their ranch. They said they were breaking their promise to Eddie, but that the day he left, he rode to their place. They let him spend the night and tried to convince him to come back and face up, telling him it had been a fair fight, that the teacher had started it. At that time he thought he had killed a man. Eddie refused their advice and headed up Strawberry with a pack wrapped in oilcloth tied behind his saddle.

The Martins were devastated. Ma retreated into her shell. All the family felt ashamed. When it was evident that the teacher would not die, there was no way to get the information to Eddie. The family knew him well enough to figure he was hiking the mountain. The clear water in Strawberry Creek provided good drinking. About halfway to the lake, hikers would cross the onion fields. The new shoots would have made good eating to go with any game Eddie killed. His .22 rifle hung to the side of his saddle on the right. It was lightweight and handy. Game was plentiful as the mountain was steep and hard climbing, not too easy for hunters. In their hearts the Martins knew how well Eddie could manage. He always had a pack ready, loved to hunt, carried two knives and a whetstone to sharpen them.

Evelyn knew something else. Eddie saved all the money he earned at various jobs. Instead of the bank, he kept a stash under his mattress. His sister knew it would be gone. She was glad because he would be able to buy things he needed when he hit a town at the end of summer. Evelyn was also sure he would roam the mountain until bad weather drove him down the other side.

Strawberry Lake was famous for trout fishing. Old Man Jones had packed in a boat that he left on the corner of the lake, protected under an outcropping of rocks. Eddie would enjoy trout more than ground squirrels or jack rabbits. If other riders came to the area, he would have to keep his horse from whinnying. Evelyn always hoped he could keep ahead of anyone sent to hunt for him by moving to Little Strawberry, Slide Lake, or High Lake. A dear or mountain goat would be too large to kill and dress out without leaving tracks. The longer he was gone, the happier she was that he was not captured. The sadder she was that she could not see her favorite brother.

Before she died, Ma received a letter that said Eddie was safe, but that he would not be returning. There was no return address and instructions inside said to burn it so it would never be traced. Evelyn watched her mother put it in the kitchen fire box. The family quit mentioning his name. Eddie was gone. That was nearly twenty-five years ago. Evelyn thought she was the only one who ever thought of him.

Nigel sat on the couch, muddy boots dirtying the rug on the floor in front of him. Evelyn ignored how tired he looked as she said, "You will never guess what Bertha Collins told me today! She and her husband may have seen Eddie at a restaurant in Nebraska while on their trip."

Nigel's voice boomed in its gravelly way. "For God's sake, Ev, give up on that runaway brother of yours. I am sick of hearing about him. You remember him as a little girl would, not as the man who deserted his responsibilities. He could be here helping to run this ranch. I could sure use some more manpower around here." With that, he rose from the couch and stomped out to the barn. Evelyn drove her memories back into her heart, but she did not let them die. Evelyn believed her brother was alive, and that thought gave her comfort.

EDDIE

Unnerved by recognizing the Collinses as customers in the Blue Cup Diner where he worked, Eddie, who called himself Jim Drake, hurried home to the house he rented with his wife Kathleen. They had met a few years before the war. Of course Eddie, the kid who liked to mix it up with his brothers back in Prairie City, volunteered to take on the Germans in France. He trained and arrived in Europe with the first American troops. Eddie had anticipated rifle shots and target shooting. Instead he found himself crawling in the mud to avoid an area where the troops were being gassed. Some of the guys got it full force, but Eddie only slightly.

A British detachment arrived to help treat the wounded. Eddie remembered Captain Smithworth, who directed the treatment with pure oxygen. Some men did not recover, but others were very grateful to Smithworth and his treatment. Eddie was shipped home due to the Captain's recommendation. He often wondered if Captain Harry Smithworth had survived the fighting.

Kathleen was expecting a baby in a couple of months. She and Jim Drake would be making a home here in Nebraska. Memories of Prairie City, Strawberry Mountain, and his sister Evelyn were pushed to the back of his mind, a twenty-five year-old secret never to be shared.

A NOTE FROM THE AUTHOR

When I discovered a packet of letters written by Harry and saved in a small red box, my historical imagination was so tweaked, that I knew I would make them the basis of my second novel in the Strawberry Mountain Series. The first in the series, *By the River,* was the story of the Martin family, inspired by information from the story of the Manwaring Wagon Trail that arrived in the John Day Valley in 1869.

Secrets from the Little Red Box is set in the early 1900s and centers around the youngest Martin daughter, Evelyn. I have changed the names from those of the real characters because the story is only my imagination of what could have happened. I made an effort to be true to the time and setting and wish I could give thanks to Harry, the primary source of my imagination.

I look at life as a series of connections, some kept, some broken, but all worth sharing in a story.

Please watch for the third novel in the Strawberry Mountains Series, *The Annie Martin Stories,* coming in 2017.

ALSO BY JAE CARVEL

By the River (Historical Fiction) Sarah Ann, a widow with three young children, arrives in the John Day Valley of Eastern Oregon in 1869, where she eventually leaves her stoic nature behind and becomes a woman of substance.

Made in the USA
Middletown, DE
21 June 2017